Tell Me a Story

Chase Collins

Tell Me a Story

• •

Shaping Your Child's Future Through Bedtime Stories

Authors Choice Press
New York Lincoln Shanghai

Tell Me A Story
Shaping Your Child's Future Through Bedtime Stories

Copyright © 1992, 2007 by Chase Collins

Authors Choice Press
an imprint of iUniverse, Inc.

iUniverse books may be ordered through booksellers or by contacting:

iUniverse
2021 Pine Lake Road, Suite 100
Lincoln, NE 68512
www.iuniverse.com
1-800-Authors (1-800-288-4677)

Because of the dynamic nature of the Internet, any Web addresses
or links contained in this book may have changed
since publication and may no longer be valid.

The views expressed in this work are solely those of the author and do not
necessarily reflect the views of the publisher, and the publisher hereby
disclaims any responsibility for them.

Originally published by Houghton Mifflin Company

ISBN: 978-0-595-46298-8 (pbk)
ISBN: 978-0-595-90852-3 (cloth)

Printed in the United States of America

Acknowledgments

To my generous and loving father and mother. To my grandparents and pioneer ancestors, to muses, Persephone, fairy tales, myths, and dreams. To the ties of love that bind us together, to trees and the open air. To canary-yellow fishes in the coral, the specific sparrows in the grass, to Grimm's, books, and lassitude. To fingernails and tears, to the fragrance of gardenias, to bumblebees and lilacs, gravestones, and letters that come in the mail. To Duncan Littlefair, to candlelight, to Dickens, to mourning. To spring, roots, and the vernal equinox. To universities and teachers and Louise Eisendrath. To poets, craft, and snippets of ribbon. To silk and diamonds and mud and tennis shoes.

To breasts and blood and bone and body. To light-ning bugs and Lake Michigan with shooting stars. To fireworks and punctuation! To language, ink, paper, energy, and music. To keys and towers, to twirling, breezed curtains, open doors, and the full moon out-side. To food and cooks, gardeners and shovels and bulbs, to computers and automobiles and wagons and tricycles and the wheel in general. To sport and ele-gance, to beauty and aging and puberty. To innocence and loss, to thought and sensation, to sleep and to heal-ing, to toothpaste and soap, to walking sticks and luna moths. To listening. To cats, ladybugs, mice, and the migrations of geese. To the telephone and washing ma-chine. To blue eyes, brown eyes, hazel eyes, and vi-sion. To breathing and holding it. To the sunburned sunset, to the sand in your shoes, to lobster, sparklers, and grilled food. To corn on the cob, the color green, the smell of coffee, the sound of another's true heart beating beneath your ear. To tender friends, to grace and gratitude, to desire, patience, and forgiveness. To Liz, Penny, and Debby, to John and Chris and their beautiful children. To the art of Melinda, Elizabeth, Janet, and Sharon. To my steady, handsome husband, Mark, his family, and of course, to my children, my inspirations: Collin, Jakeson, and Gwane.

Contents

8. Style, Detail, and Burrs 116

9. Symbols (Bong) and How to Make Them 127

10. Happy Endings 150

Tell Me a Story

◆ Who are you going to believe,
some silly writer or a real tiger?
— "Hobbes" (Bill Watterson)

1

Yes, You Can

◆ ◆ THE PURPOSE of this book is to refresh in you the creative confidence you were born with, to call it up again for the sake of the most important new person in the world: your child. It is about understanding your youngster and the free spirit within you, about imagination and its sources, and about the nuts and bolts of the classic tale. With some reassuring outlines of the good basic story, some ideas and concepts about the process, I believe you will find the courage and desire to invent stories of your own.

And when you do, you will discover you have an old-new way to profoundly communicate with and encourage your child, to shape his or her outlook on the future. Storytelling gives you the power to express what you know in the most interesting way, to express your love, hope, concern, knowledge, understanding, and experience in the most palatable form — a way that takes you above and beyond the constant parental juggling act of explanations, discipline, good examples, cajolery, lectures, and whatever else works.

Mark Twain once quipped that he had received public schooling as a child but never let it interfere with his education. Children today — stuck in a society of troubled schools, distant Nature, changing family relationships, and a diminishing sense of control over problems — have lost some of the old assurances that used to encourage them in growing up. And we parents, you and I, occasionally lie awake at night, thinking futile thoughts about the globe, wondering what one puny human being can do about it all.

I say, in this uncertain world, start at home. Start in your area of competence with things you can affect. Start with love — not abstract, heroic, frustrated love for planet, nation, the next generation, but rather love for the humble, anonymous, promising, rewarding glory of your own child. With storytelling, I believe you can help *one* young child succeed in growing up with confidence. Your conviction that your child *will* succeed is what he or she needs most to be able to do so. With no pretensions about global solutions, tell generous, encouraging, caring stories to your children about the life they are living.

The purpose of your story is to tell your child that you are convinced that he or she will succeed in the task of growing up, that you believe your child embodies the mental, physical, and emotional lights needed in the lifelong search for that elusive, consoling treasure we call "meaning." Equally vital, but more spirited than "meaning," you believe your child's future will include, as Joseph Campbell put it, "the rapture of being alive."

In the modern arsenal of parental tactics, there lingers in storytelling a powerful communicative art. Storytelling is a beautiful, infinitely variable simplicity often buried or forgotten under all the other, fancy childraising stuff. This book is intended to help resurrect this artifact of all cultures, this charged, creative remnant, to polish it up a bit and make it shine again, through you.

Children love to listen to stories. When you tell a good one, you have a very sympathetic audience, listening hard. As you start, you should know that your child wants you to succeed and believes you can. Don't fret that you cannot immediately come up with something as enduring as "Hansel and Gretel"; then again, you have no way of knowing if one of your tales might not become a baby "Cinderella."

Your children will be touched to have you affirm the imaginative world they live in, and you will show them that, along with all the facts, you also see some magic in the universe. Children believe there is a place for enchantment in our everyday lives, and as you create stories for your children, you honor it and them. In this land of imagination — this world of the possible — your children will understand you are indeed the good king or queen they believe you are.

I think I can make you feel comfortable as the person in the seemingly foolish star-covered hat. You are the storyteller, the fabler, the spinner of fantasies you never thought you were. You still have some hocus-pocus in you. You can pull out your dream-maker from the middle of your adult clutter and kindle that imaginative fire you once used so often as a child. Your imagination never really leaves you, no matter how scattered, distracted, and tizzed you are during the day. There is a time — bedtime — to pull it all together and make up a story, right on the spot. Not only are you capable of doing it, but I hope to persuade you that it is very necessary to *your* happiness, to *your* sense of aliveness, to do it. Even as you know that life is difficult and sometimes disappointing, every time you tell a story you will find — as I have — that you inch forward in your own search for meaning, vitality, the gist of it all.

Storytelling, like learning how to "pump" on a swing, is a matter of finding the force, energy, and delight you were born with. Once you've learned how to kick up your heels, you'll never be left hanging. Once you've got your weight behind storytelling, got the rhythm of it, know when to bend and when to stretch, you and your child are ready to swing up, out, and back again on what will become one of the most memorable, freeing, exhilarating experiences of your lives. Rainy days, ice storms, frayed ropes will never stop you; in fact, they will inspire you in the quiet art of storytelling.

For you and for your children, something wonderful will happen when you quietly say, "Once upon a time . . ."

- ◆ Behold the turtle. He makes progress only when he sticks his neck out.
  — *James Bryant Conant*

- ◆ Our chief want in life is somebody who shall make us do what we can.
  — *Ralph Waldo Emerson*

2

You Are Creative and You've Always Known It

◆ ◆ SHORTLY AFTER my first baby was born, I realized I had come down with a bad case of mental confetti. The infant who had done this to me was, no question, adorable, but she got sick on my birthday, besmirched my career clothes, overwhelmed everything. Time itself was the first to fall. The teakettle melted down on the stove, the rubber nipples scorched, I ate ice cream at three in the morning, I lost my beat for jokes. In my rush and forgetfulness, I couldn't scrape together enough time to shower *and* wash my hair: hearing one squawk, I was on duty, toweled, cribside. A month or so in, sleep had become a foreign city. Just getting out the front door was a victory. I could not sustain a thought but pretended to, which took considerable energy.

At six months, I was running on empty, tearing through the market, a picture of frazzled competence. I never forgot the diapers, flashed past time-wasters — hair conditioner, silver polish, newspapers — and repeatedly patted my pockets to be sure I had the keys. I tried to keep a perspective on what mattered. The only things on my calendar which couldn't be changed were the days the baby-sitter was off. One year in, I began to make worrying into an art form: the corners on the coffee table, the swallowability of paper clips, Drano, dust bunnies. My back hurt, but everything I could lift was four feet up, toddler-safe. I had vowed I'd never consider a playpen, an amusing, purist philosophy. My husband wanted a vacation alone with me; I wasn't even flattered. We'd talk about nothing but the child anyway — why travel? At the same time, I bemoaned the lost conversational continents of politics, history, sex, art, business, sports, movies, theater, ideas. "Parenting" had become a pip-squeak of a term, too manageable-sounding, too do-able, lacking that squirt of life and death, pinched fingers, about-face, right-nowness that real child care was about. "Love" seemed inarticulate too. "Having" a baby was supposed to mean birth. Two years later, my brain with a thousand new synapses, I knew it was a lifetime and couldn't imagine a day without my wonderful little girl.

When she was two, we were both ready for story-telling. Somehow the jammed schedules and mad dashes had become less harrowing. Now that she was old enough to listen to a story, not just wiggle over a word book, things changed: time ticked with a slower, deeper awareness. Who knows whether it was she or I who changed, but after two years of astounding mutual distractibility, I had a child who could understand basic language — even if she couldn't speak it perfectly herself — and knew the names of emotions as well as colors, things, people, and who, when we took a walk, could call out such esoterica as "butterfly" and "toadstool."

One night, exhausted to the bone, I found myself dreading a part of our bedtime routine: my chipper bending and twisting over the bookcase to assist in her choice of books, my having to sit up and support both our bodies with a reading of two or three favorites, and finally my sore back's effort to lovingly hoist her increasingly heavy weight over the crib bars and down to the mattress for the night. All I wanted to do was lie down, immediately. The "big girl" bed, awaiting her graduation to the next stage, sat there in the room like forbidden fruit.

I told her I had a wonderful surprise for her, but she had to be in the crib first. That done, I dimmed the lights, lay down on the welcome bed, reached my hand to hers and, holding it, told her a story. Flat on my back, I made it up. She listened for a full, motionless five minutes. Yes. Five. The story seemed to come out of thin air. I decided then and there that I would do it again. She had been deeply interested; I had so enjoyed it.

Storytelling Is Good for You

In addition to the physical relief (need I say more?), storytelling is an emotional and intellectual release, which is a bit more complicated. After my first child was born, my capacity to love went up by about a third. I'd already loved my parents, my siblings, my friends, my husband, but never before had I experienced the powerhouse, the wham, the earthquake of love I felt for my own young. Storytelling draws on this new capacity within you — to love, to work, to live — and brings it to physical, hearable, sharable form. Simply put, storytelling is a wonderful release for all this energy. It's relaxing for *you*. It takes that remarkable new third in you and sends it out in a usable, satisfying way, bringing an intensely welcome sense of accomplishment and completion, something you need now more than ever.

And it brings a strange kind of peace to the teller to make up a story. It slows you down, draws your mind away from the mental confetti and into a dreamland where all you have to do is what pleases you, what interests you, what occurs to you. Deep in the story, your mind reaches another place, serene yet alert, curious and adventurous and honest, a picture land, half memory, half fancy. Because you know your child is listening, your mind comes as close to childlike as it can get. You see colors as children do, want to touch the things that children reach for. Deep in the story, you reenter the mind of a child. Oh, how can I tell you so that you will believe me! It is beautiful, vibrant, glowing, miraculous, divine to be deep in a story! It is a restorative, a vacation. It refreshes like cool water, deep sleep, long kisses, a good laugh, tears, joy.

Children Remember the Tale Bearers

If someone told you stories in your young life, no doubt you remember those moments. I'm not talking about the family anecdotes your grandmother recounted over a game of canasta, profoundly important as those histories are, I'm referring to a clear-cut, demarcated period of time when it was declared that this was a *story* being told. A formal acknowledgment. Children instinctively appreciate those moments and know they are rare.

If those times when someone told you a story were delicious and sweet, I'm delighted for you. But if, thinking back, you recall some story as disappointing or obvious, you probably still remember the teller with fondness. And if you remember the story was worse than a flop, was inept, dreadful, and cautionary *(Once upon a time there was a little girl who wouldn't stop sucking her thumb, so Strumpelpeter cut it off)*, don't be daunted. You certainly can improve upon such an ignorant tale. If your memories of storytelling are ambivalent, tell a story anyway. Just don't make the same mistakes that were made with you.

Unfortunately, very few of us have any memories whatsoever of being told stories. This precious activity is dying out in favor of television, videos, Nintendo, the electronic stimulations in our homes that fill the time once spent in human company. Many of us were raised with these gadgets too, giving us less direct, personal memory with which to reverse the trend.

Long ago, when sundown brought out candles instead of computer games, people entertained one another. When it was dark, there was the light of other people, the light of imagination in the child's home. People talked to one another or sat together at the hearth and watched the fire. In the company of the hypnotically flowing blue and orange flames, the whispering and crackling sounds, minds drifted and stories were told.

Now, this is not to say that I'm against the modern world. In fact, my children have all of the doodads I've mentioned, and then some. We occasionally squabble about too much TV, and I sometimes give in because I have work to do, and it is easier. But I know that after they watch TV, I can also tell a story. I haven't left my child's developing mind up to the networks or the tiny beeping screens. With storytelling, I maintain something creatively precious in our family in spite of other entertainments and distractions. Stories still fit the modern screen of life and enhance it, as they always have.

Storytelling Is Tailor-made Caring

One day my three-year-old son and I drove through a car wash. As we rolled into the dark tunnel, hissing sprays hit the side, and bubbling trails drooled down the gloomy windows all around us. Then came the deluge, pummeling, roaring overhead, and monstrous gray rags — mechanically licking and waving and sinking — came upon us like an insatiable beast. My son was terrified.

Did I have the inclination to run him through the tunnel a few more times just to prove to him that he would not die there? Of course not. Did I have a book about a car wash in the back seat, written and ready to go, with glorious illustrations showing that there was nothing to be afraid of? No. Could I count on Mr. Rogers to address the subject when we got home? No again. Mr. Rogers was singing about fear of drains that day.

Of course the first thing I did was comfort, hold, and explain to my son, very simply and truthfully: we're safe here, the windshield won't break, the raggedy arms of cloth and the scrubber-brushes are not monsters. But my straightforward explanation of car wash mechanics could hardly address the much more important fact of my son's experience: he was scared, he felt powerless, helpless, and threatened. He needed to feel there was something he could do to save himself and had no idea what it was. These emotions are profound and human and deeply important.

That night I made up a story that addressed those helpless feelings he had in abundance. I created a tale that not only instructed him about the reality of the car wash but also showed him how well I understood and loved him. With a story about a mouse named Feathersack — a familiar character in my stories — I let him know that he wasn't powerless. I told him symbolically that his brain and body would sustain him and help him succeed in growing up, facing his fears.

Once upon a time there was a dear little mouse

named Feathersack who lived way down deep in a big bag of feathers in a pillow factory. One day when she was out walking, she decided to explore a tunnel, a dark opening, in a building down the street.

The thing that really caught her eye was the beautiful silver road that ran down the middle of it, glowing from light at the other end. The silver road was raised up, almost like a little wall, and just perfect for high-up walking and looking down on things. Feathersack balanced with her tail and began to tightrope. Suddenly, tremendous, roaring water came on, and Feathersack was tossed around in the gale of the car wash, rolled and somersaulted and drenched. It was awful.

Behind her, the undersides of a car moved as mechanically as the rags, hooked by a chain to her silver road. Would she be run over? Would she be drowned? She scrambled up under the fender of the car for shelter, hoping the monster-rags couldn't find her there. She could see better.

She spotted, high up on the wall, an electric switch with two lights on it. The green one was on. The red one was dark. She thought, "Switches mean machines."

That gave her courage. She dashed from under the car, scampered up the metal cable that ran to the switch, and, leaping on it with her paws, pulled it down with all her might. The red light — almost as big as her face — came on, and instantly the machine stopped and the rags hung dripping and stupid in the rainy air.

Feathersack, quite shaky and wet outside — but victorious inside — jumped down and ran like mad. The sun was so bright outside that she blinked, then *sneezed. A man came, shouting, "Who did that! Who turned it off?"*

But Feathersack didn't say a word. She just smiled, shook the water from her fur, and hurried home. She was completely dry when she got there and very happy indeed to see her own room again, just as she had left it.

Now, you may be thinking that you can't make up a story as detailed as this. You really can. Although it has taken me years to develop my style of storytelling, I want you to know that I intend to spill the beans on all I've discovered in order to make *your* efforts fruitful in far less time than it took me. You *can* tell a story like this. I'll show you how, but for now what is most important to know is this: storytelling creates a powerful bond between you and your child. Storytelling is an act of caring. My son knew that my love for him had prompted the story. A child senses that it is more personal to spin a tale about his concerns than to distract him with a cookie, more productive than just dabbing at his tears and pooh-poohing their cause, and definitely more fun for both of you. In a story, you speak to your child in a language that is understood instinctively: the language of the imagination. You are showing him in the most entertaining way that he has the power to face difficulties and grow in understanding.

"Why Make Up Stories When There Are Already So Many Good Books?"

Books are written for children in general, while your story is for one child in particular, a person unlike any you've ever known before or ever will know again. Your child needs both books and the stories you invent. This combination in your child's life is a perfect mix, a surf 'n' turf combo that is sure to please everyone and promote richer understanding all around. No question, reading books to your children is a superb way to get them started on the joy of the printed page; they will want to read if they have been read to, and wise parents give their children a leg up on literacy by reading aloud as early as possible. As Mark Twain said, "Those who do not read good books have no advantage over those who can't."

But in many situations a book is not as good as a homemade story. Once children begin to know the names of things, they are on to the next stage: understanding their experiences. The wealth of experience, the zillions of mundane fragments that happen to your child during one single day, cannot possibly be addressed by your juvenile library — there aren't enough books in the world! The smallest things can trigger great and useful stories: perhaps your child notices the smooth-shaven affection of Daddy's morning cheek compared to his whiskery evening smooches; or sees the spoon fished out of the garbage disposal, misshapen; or spends an hour strumming a twanging note on the screen door spring-closer; or grips the remnants of a popped birthday balloon; or wonders at a cardinal in the snow-covered tree; or endures the burn of jealousy as an older child gets to go down the slide completely alone. These are inspirations for stories, and, as with the car wash, you may not have *that* book on hand. Grand-scale experiences are always worthy too: the first visit to the echoing lion house at the zoo or the dairy barn where fifty cows nearly overwhelmed you both with the physical sense of "herd." These just holler for a good yarn. Thousands of things happen each day that only you — knowing your child better than anyone else — can address.

As Bruno Bettelheim says in his book *The Good Enough Parent:* "No book can encompass the millions of problems that may be encountered in child-rearing, nor the unlimited variations in which they can manifest themselves. For his own sake, and that of his child, a parent must solve problems as they occur and in his very own way; otherwise, his solution will fit neither him nor his child, nor will he feel good about it." My way of explaining problems and experiences as they occur with my children has been to use them as springboards for stories. When I invest myself — my nature, ideas, images, and experience — and my love and knowledge of my child in a story, it comes very close indeed to the core of my child's being. In stories, I communicate on another level, a level where my child is very much at ease, perhaps more at ease in his young life than with a book. Few books can be targeted at a unique moment in my child's life as well as my own tale.

And books do not grow with the child. They are always and forever pegged into an age level that cannot be adjusted. Your stories, on the other hand, are completely adjustable. Although reading a book your child has outgrown intellectually may be very pleasant and soothing, like being with an old friend, it does not ask your child to stretch beyond the momentary pleasure of hearing it. Your stories can always encourage your child to stretch because you make them for that very purpose, to affirm that your child will, so to speak, improve with age.

Most important, your stories can be aimed exactly at that very distinct, individual person your child is. Telling a bedtime story is the most personal, profound way to encourage that miraculous, subtle, specifically freckled human being you know so well. No book can match your "feel" for your child.

And for you, storytelling will also become an expression of the freedom, the creativity, the playfulness of your parental mind. Storytelling is a ranging art, a truly limitless, generous, caring craft. It comes from your sense of openness to your child's life and is full of your love and concern for him, start to finish.

"Is It Hard to Match Stories to My Child's Stage of Development?"

Childhood development is a sweeping vista, as you well know, or soon will. From my reading and personal experience, here are some snapshots of the terrain. English is the only language in which the personal pronoun "I" is capitalized, and two- and three-year-olds, having discovered the primacy of the word, embrace it thoroughly. Insatiably, they want to explore their self-awareness — tasting, touching, smelling, hearing, seeing, learning about their physical existence — and they don't care much about others. In the "I"-land, two- and three-year-olds naturally play next to — not with — other children. They are also adamantly independent; as my two-and-a-half-year-old daughter Gwane shouted at me when I leaned to put her shoe on her foot, "*I* ou (will) do it, *I* ou do it!"

By three years old, the "I" has occasionally become "we," and getting dressed has primarily become *what* to wear, not who will do it. (This stage lasts and intensifies through adolescence!) Three will give a running commentary on his or her every motion, pretend to tell time, hold up three akimbo fingers for "How old are you?" — but if you skip one page of a favorite book, three will set you straight with the stern finger of a professor. Two was in love with the parents, three asked them for help, but four has an inkling that they are imperfect beings. The four-year-old will quickly push aside the pat-the-bunny book and be interested in such sophistication as dinosaurs or poems like "Jabberwocky" or "Custard, the Cowardly Dragon." While toddlers need to be diverted more often than disciplined, the four-year-old sometimes welcomes control; when my daughter Collin was asked by her younger cousin Sarah how she managed to stop sucking her thumb, she replied, "It's simple. Just get your daddy to make you a rule."

Children playing together at five can be quite sociable, exchanging quips, getting a kick out of wacky word play, or making considerate gestures back and forth. School has arrived, and when the schoolboy assesses the weather, he may say, "Now, *this* is a great day for recess." Five is much more likely than three to say,

"This is my lucky day!" Five-year-olds ask why incessantly. (I was one mother who loved it.) Six is reading, probably, can count to twenty, and has achieved a mysterious individuality that cannot be tracked in so neat a way as two to five. By seven, the entire body has replaced itself, cell by cell; no wonder these children are mysterious as never before — seven is all new! But a child of seven, eight, nine, ten, even eleven, having outgrown so many stages, still wants to hear your invented stories.

In storytelling, one sturdy rope — animism — lasts through each of these spiraling, multileaved developmental stages. Animism is the attitude that all things have souls or consciousness very much as we do. It is an idea that appeals all the way to puberty. In the world of imagination — no matter how old the child is — a lion, a balloon, a slide, or a whisker can talk. What the whisker *says*, however, must be age-appropriate. When telling stories, you won't really find this so hard to do. When you go into a bookstore, you usually know which book is about right for your child's ability. In the same way, you will instinctively know how to adapt your stories to your child's development. The simplest route is to take an actual experience of the day as your subject matter, "animate" it creatively (I'll say more about this in a few pages), and tell the story with the usual, daily vocabulary. Your whisker will speak appropriately.

"But I'm Not Creative"

You say you are not creative, and you think it's true, but if you will keep an open mind for a few paragraphs here, I hope you will come to a different sort of conclusion about yourself, a more fitting one.

Before getting into helpful hints on creativity, let me shoot straight from the hip. Telling stories to your child does not require an overwhelming amount of creativity. You have enough.

I submit that in your very most secret self you believe you *are* creative — you've always known it — but you just don't know how to use what you have. Let's give that last sentence a ten-second bit of air space; if this were radio, there'd be an airy instrument breathing an inner melody while you ponder, secretly, am I creative?

Once, you never questioned your creativity. Go back to square one, to the time when you vaguely remember coming to your "poor me, I'm not creative" conclusion. Just before that crucial moment when the stone curtain of Noncreativity dropped with a crash on your toes, did anyone happen to say, "Oops, hold the curtain! I forgot to tell you. That little thingy you made is disappointing, but creativity is a process! Try again!" No one said it? A Large Omission, for truly, creativity *is* the process of discovering the good poem in the mess of words, searching out the telling drawing within the scribbles, finding the true shape hidden within the already pinched and globby clay. You have to try it again. A failed drawing, a flop of a sculpture, or a lousy poem is not the lack of creativity, it is the lack of the sustained creative process. No one mentioned that creativity is an incremental, step-by-step sort of thing? Hmmm. Would you entertain the thought that your poem may have been truly crummy, but your creativity wasn't?

Well, let's try this. Probably no one told you that creativity is not really prodigious talent, but an attitude toward the question posed. The second Large Omission. The creative mind restates the question. Creativity is a way of bending, twisting, and reexamining questions from another edge or vantage point. There's a great illustrative story from NASA. The team was trying to find a material that could protect the astronauts from the tremendous, metal-melting heat of reentry. It was impossible until they rephrased the problem. The new goal was not to create a metal that could take it entirely undamaged but to find a metal that could take it long enough, melting all the way, for the spaceship to get through uncooked.

Every single day, when dealing with your child's behavior, you practice this kind of rephrasing, this "thinking on the edge." It is a parental survival tactic of the first rank. Taking a different tack, thinking tangentially, spontaneously altering your approach, is something you are quite familiar with because you do it daily with your child.

And finally, did anyone suggest that creativity has to do with being prepared? Now, don't get a nervous stomach; I don't mean prepared in the sense of having your homework completed, your outline highlighted in yellow, your speech on note cards, math formulas down pat, and white-out in your pocket, but rather *prepared* to willingly receive some fleeting thought, some last-minute escape hatch; prepared to put your foot on some serendipitous bridge in the fog that turns out to be draped with morning glories and leads to exactly the right place. Favoring the waiting, expectant, miscellaneous mind, creativity is enjoying the *means*, the wandering, the spontaneity of the moment. It is ready to receive something out of the blue. It does not shoot for the end goal; it can always punt.

This book is preparing you, right now, to accept and act on your creativity. You are building it as you read. In sum, creativity is an outgrowth of sustained process, rephrasing, and readiness. These are the more or less ordinary tools we use for "regular" work. That fact should calm your nerves a bit.

Now let's get down to some scholarly brass tacks. Howard Gardner, Professor of Education at Harvard and co-director of Project Zero — a project to study creativity and the nature of intelligence, as well as the state of communicable knowledge in art education — says there are seven different kinds of intelligence. (Note, as I did, that he uses the word "intelligence" here.) A couple of them are obvious to us terrestrials — math/logic and language — but he also includes five other kinds of intelligence in his list: music, spatial (painting and sculpture), body kinesthetic (dance), understanding others, and self-understanding. Gardner maintains that each of us possesses a unique blend of all seven kinds of intelligence.

You probably have some SAT scores in the back of your mind; put them aside. Those tests measure only the linguistic and mathematical-logical kinds of intelligence and none of the others. Now, this is important: how would you measure yourself on the *other* forms of intelligence? If someone said, "Can you dance?" you would probably say, "Yes, when my favorite song comes on." If someone asked, "Do you understand other people?" you would give yourself a partial score and say, "Yes, I understand most of them pretty well." If asked, "Do you understand yourself?" you would answer with some confidence that you've been working on it. The point is that on "other" sorts of intelligence, you'd give yourself mixed scores, not total zeros. Do the same with storytelling.

Develop your born-in creativity by taking a less blanket, defeatist attitude; be curious, patient, friendly, and nurturing toward it. The degree to which you *use* what you have determines how muscular or winged or stunted it is. Now, I'm not saying that creativity is the same for everyone; there is genius-level creativity and there's the level you and I have. But Gardner makes another very crucial point about creativity. He says, "You have to *want* to be creative." Put this foremost in your mind. *There is no way of knowing that you are creative until you wish to be.*

David Perkins, Gardner's colleague and co-director of Project Zero, adds that all creative people share one characteristic: a drive to reduce complexity to order and simplicity. With all humility and respect to you, Mr. Perkins, I say that every galloping, ragged parent in the world seeks order and simplicity, especially after spending some time with a tired three-year-old. To some degree, therefore, we parents are all creative. We soon learn that children shun the parent's idea of creative clothing, are not served by the parent's creative automobile driving, and emphatically do not eat creative food. They are, however, enchanted by creative storytelling. Your child will respond to your newfound creativity, will be buoyed by your use of it, and in some wonderful, mysterious way it will make you a better parent.

So the only real stumbling block to telling stories is not your lack of creativity but your willingness to give it a few rounds and a breath of fresh air. Yes, it is open-ended and mysterious, and yes, storytelling requires that you trust your creativity. But since creative intelligence is born in, everyone still has it, and with a certain tending, it stays with us all our lives, and improves. It takes spontaneity, curiosity, boldness, a sense of adventure to explore it — but, believe it or not, you have a wide view, a huge ranch, a panorama of creativity if you visualize yourself as having it. Now is the time for you to *want* to be creative, and confidence-building doors will swing open to you. If you are afraid that your imagination will spurt up horrible things, scaring you and your child, read on. There are boundaries to the basic tale, as I see it, that will protect you from making that mistake. The structure of the story, in my "Nitty-Gritty" Chapter 6, will prevent wild imaginings from running away with you.

"But I'm Too Tired"

In spite of all that goes on during a day — the mad dashes, the jammed schedules, the mental confetti — at the end of the day you will find that a remarkable new energy fills you as you anticipate telling a story. It is a quiet, connected sort of energy, partly derived, I think, from your child's desire to hear a story. This energy will help you devise a tale that will charm your child and explain a very particular event in your child's life.

Fatigue is the most common excuse for not trying. Truly I understand if you say, "I'm so exhausted after the day, if I have to do one more thing before bedtime, I'll collapse." Well then, I say (this is experience talking), go ahead, collapse! Lie down in your child's room and let your exhaustion flatten you. You will discover that, for the most part, your exhaustion is physical. As you "collapse" you will find that your mind is still buzzing. Don't be afraid to let your thoughts whirl: whiz down the musts of tomorrow's grocery shopping, the appointments, video returns, social obligations, children's shoes to be bought, the missing gym clothes, deadlines, whose birthday is coming up, the peas your child squirreled in his napkin at dinner.

Go ahead and drift for a few seconds, drift and reach for your creativity, drift and *want* to be imaginative. To your surprise, I believe, you will discover that your imagination stirs. There could be story material in that buzz: perhaps a story about the cow that followed her milk all the way to the store, the gym clothes that played hide-and-seek, the lamb who couldn't keep the secret about the surprise party. You too may pass on the peas, but somewhere in your list may be a clicker of a story, and your child is looking forward to it. I'll be talking very soon about more ways to really get your imagination rolling.

"But I Have Nothing to Say"

If you are still unsure of yourself, then you've got what I call a personally invented, this-nag's-for-you, sneering internal critic. Let's name him — unfondly — Bertyl, after a teacher I once had: the jugular, mortifying margin-blaster of my youthful enthusiasms.

This voice, this Bertyl, will come to you at unwelcome moments — for instance, when you consider making all your Christmas or Hanukkah gifts, running for local office, constructing a sled out of skis and a laundry basket, writing a letter to the editor of the *New York Times*, or inventing a story. Bertyl will tell you you can't do it, you're no good.

By now, Bertyl's denigrating voice may be so familiar, so ingrained, that it sounds just like your own true one and manages, in a flash, to beat your confidence to a pulp. Your Bertyl is a niggling, negative, belittling voice that may have started in the back of your head when a scowling teacher with long black hairs on his arms began to assault your papers with a red pen, madly circling your misspellings, scribbling "huh?" next to the paragraph you thought was pretty funny or original, putting that hideous "awk" next to the beautiful word you loved. Or perhaps it was your well-intentioned parents, siblings, or friends who pick pick picked at your joyous confidence until you became an easy-road perfectionist and your creativity became a dinky, wizened little shame:

"So what if it's descriptive, there is no 'z' in 'surprise.' "

"What's *that* a picture of?"

Sadly, too many of us bow before Bertyl and smother our sense of being dreamy, surprising, inspired people. And Bertyl can blab on for years, goading our worst adult fears:

"You can't do it, you're too old."

"Don't you have something important to do?"

"Watch out! Make a stupid mistake and you'll ruin your child forever!"

Your know-it-all critic makes you self-conscious, hesitant, timid. You're left always looking over your shoulder, asking, "How'm I doin', how'm I doin'?" Bertyl is very effective. You cave in.

Why? Because it is easier not to try to be dashingly, energetically imaginative. We're so browbeaten we no longer listen to the pure, living, creative voice within us.

What we all need, you and I, when we venture into the land of storytelling, is to listen to another voice behind Bertyl's, not a critic, but the voice of the Good Teacher we might have had, the one who adores us, thinks we are remarkably alive, *hilarious*, believes in our tender, free-spirited, whoopee imaginativeness. Who says, "You are talented, terrific, gifted, original! Go to it!"

Let Bertyl advise when you consider, for instance, skydiving. But get rid of him at storytime. Trust your creativity as you did when you were a child. Trust that you do have something to say. Trust that you will have enough energy left over from the day to tell a story. You really do have everything you need: the day's events, your desire to do it, and your love for your child.

♦ I listen to the voices.
    — *William Faulkner*

3

Fire, Embers, Lamps, Spontaneous Combustion, and Starlight: Your Local Muses

♦ ♦ ADMITTING YOU HAVE some ill-developed, rudi-
mentary, fetal creativity is not the same thing as being
confident you can stand up, flap your wings, and use
it. You may not feel you're ready yet.

In order to get you there, I am going to stay close to
you for this next chapter. I do this not only to support
your fledgling spirits but also to proceed from where
stories really originate: in you, in your heart and

mind. We are starting at home base, the crux of it all, with you and your observations about your child.

In the next few pages you will become better acquainted with your muses and, knowing them, will have more confidence in your creativity and insight as a storyteller. I will put you in touch, step by step, with your trusty, homegrown, local sources of inspiration. Later in the book we'll go through the stages of getting ready to invent a story: you'll fly out to the more universal realm of human imagination; you'll learn about how to recognize it in yourself, how it functions in all of us, and how to put it to use. Finally I'll get you ready for launch with the storytelling specifics on character, plot, and resolution.

But right now, in terms of your creativity, you're in that sort of childlike position of realizing, actually believing, that you have two hands, and suddenly you are terrified that someone is going to ask you to use those hands to type something spellbinding and instructive, with no mistakes. You don't know the alphabet, you don't know the words, and — worst of all — you've never seen a keyboard in your life. You don't know where to start.

Right here. We're on the lookout now for your muses, your inspirations, your idea-givers. I want you to know that these muses won't come to you from the outside, they are *in* you already. You are crawling, beaming, radiant with them, or soon will be. You may not see them all at once, but you will eventually, because they are a part of your life.

Your inner muses — emotion, memory, empathy, hunch, and ancestral memory — are those most welcome elves who will arrive in the night and turn all your straw into gold. Your muses can appear at all times, all levels, all stages of the story and in infinite constellations and combinations. Some nights one or two of them will predominate, shining like great careening searchlights crisscrossing the black sky. Some nights they work together like a herd of phosphorescent horses galloping you to remote mountain peaks, faraway castles. Some nights, when you are utterly blank and uninspired, lo and behold, one light will appear as a passing flash, a poof from a fairy match, giving you a glimpse of something to "tell" about, and before the light burns out you've got your idea. These lights are all yours; you already have them. What I hope to do is to turn them on — kindle them in you — and show you how they work in storytelling.

Think of your muses as idea-makers, magical genies, mentors, scouts, escorts, confidantes, bloodhounds sniffing out the trail of a great story. Large or small, they are glowing all around you as you leap off into the unknown.

These five are a daunting group indeed to your inner critic, who will stagger off into the dark where he belongs. Your muses will also help you find the way through the storytelling thicket, spell out motivation, take the veil off your character, clear an exciting path for you to wander with your child, and suggest endings and solutions to your stories. Overall, they guide you along the "what next" aspect of storytelling. Finally, you don't have to do anything to "earn" them, no Ph.D., no internship, no credentials; all you need is a few years of living and thinking about life. On the night you begin to tell stories, you should glance inwardly at these good friends, your muses. Without them, you will be left with what Tolstoy called "brain-spun" stories, didactic, bossy, dull things, and your listeners will nod off because they are too young to be polite. With them, both you and your child will be captivated.

The Fire of Emotion

Every story is based, for you and for your child, somewhere in emotion. Babies have simple, powerful emotions and start using them immediately to survive, using them on us. Later, as the child's emotions become more complex, they remain every bit as worthy as our own, every bit as powerful and important for survival and living. And always they are primary material for stories.

I remember the first moment I had the leisure and consciousness to inspect my newborn daughter. When they brought her to me in my hospital room, I was exhausted from giving birth, propped in bed in a silky blue and pink robe my mother had given me. With my baby's ineffable being and delicate weight freed from inside my body and at last in my arms, I looked into that utterly new face in my life, wanting to inhale it like the May morning outside. I closed my eyes and breathed. That took a few seconds; it was nice. Feeling obliged to do something more, I began the cliché routine of undressing her and counting her toes and so on. I remember feeling sadly unsatisfied with that little ritual — no goose bumps, no welling tears. Perhaps I was not going to be a good mother after all; maybe I didn't have it. I dressed her again and just looked at her face, this time not trying to do anything. There was a face I was going to know very well, I supposed. Swallowing my disappointment about the bore of her toes, what did I see? Her floating newborn, navy blue eyes, and such livingness! Quickly then I noticed that her face was just ticking with emotions. Joy, curiosity, sadness, and serenity raced across her features — emotions in fast forward, moods by a hyper puppeteer. Her eyes flashed and squinted, her mouth moved from sour to sweet, her brows carried on, her arms rose and sank in wavelike motions as if she were conducting some unheard ancient music. All this, as far as I could know, for no reason whatsoever. She was practicing emotions, I thought, the sweeping, grand ones. Now we're talking motherhood.

It did not take her long to prove to me that she was indeed feeling a good number of things that flew by her features. I came quickly to realize that my child had most of the repertoire of emotions that I did, and that in spite of tremendous differences between our experiences and knowledge, she often had me on equal emotional ground. When she sighed with pleasure, when she ranted with loneliness, when she laughed as the breeze blew through her hair, when she cooed at a toy or, even better, at *me*, I knew she felt joy and sorrow as powerfully as I did. And yes, there were times when we disagreed emotionally. I welcomed her naptime; she didn't. I thought the gruel would hit the spot in her hungry tummy; she preferred it on the floor. I thought the scratch-and-sniff book a chore; she didn't. But her *desire* to lean into a chemical-smelling picture of a pine tree was equal to my *desire* to distract her with a reading of my favorite book. Children are indeed our equals in experiencing emotion.

The current fuss about the cognitive and physical development of children often overlooks the utterly human aspect of the child's emotional awareness. Some people seem to put more emphasis on timely achievement of developmental milestones like toilet training or reading than on the child's emotional readiness for that accomplishment. I deeply believe that the emotional vocabulary precedes readiness and the rest of the child's intellectual growth. First we learn the personal meaning of "sad" and "glad," then we tackle the other stuff. And I maintain that the child's desire for the accomplishment precedes his or her ability to do it in a positive way. He or she may be manipulated or forced or rewarded into some behavior, but the victory of the accomplishment is felt only when the child desires it, not when the parents do. And the victory is what matters emotionally to the child. The child will read, really read, when his or her emotional scope takes pleasure in words and ideas more than just in the mouthing of sounds. The child will use the potty when that powerful emotional self accepts it, welcomes it.

Storytelling is a way to prepare children for emotional life. You can shape your children's future by helping them clarify the emotions they experience and by suggesting future actions and thoughts that will aid them in growing up. In a story, you can hold aside the confusing branches that fall over the path to adulthood and make it possible for your children to imaginatively see and accept their feelings and, with cumulative stories, to expand their self-confidence, intellect, vision, and courage. By being alert to your children's worries and wishes, you can suggest solutions to the dilemmas that fluster, frustrate, and hurt them. Storytelling is a superb way to honor emotions, to show how important and natural you know they are.

One thing to remember in storytelling is how pure feelings emerge. The point is not the worthiness of the object but the feeling it inspires. For instance, your awe under the Sistine Ceiling may be much like your child's awe of the flying Superman. Winning the lottery may feel just like the morning Santa comes through. A year in Florence may be the emotional equivalent of an amusement park for the afternoon. The Chinese alphabet is as confusing to you as the multiplication tables are to your child.

The parent who observes and honors the child's emotions can be forgiven lesser sins (working late into the evening, forgetting to buy Oreos, cursing when stepping barefooted on a Lego); your little failings don't matter anywhere near as much as showing understanding of your child's emotions. It is easy to pooh-pooh a child's tears over a lost toy — a toy for instance that you hated, whose noise drove you up the wall, whose concept offended you — but if he has lost his little GI Joe and is devastated, let's hear no "good riddances." What is important is not the toy but how the child feels about the loss of it. Take the word "loss" and play with it, ponder it, remember some personal loss, and you will come much closer to understanding how your child feels. While you're at it, be sure to mentally note it as story material.

And don't forget your own emotional capacity. How it has grown because of your child! Raising a child brings on a pageant, a panorama, a conflagration of emotions, and, at the same time, intense, new kinds of self-appraisal. Not only did I experience the thrill and horror of being recognized by my baby solely as a parent, but I was stopped in my tracks by what Wordsworth called "the grandeur of the beating of the human heart." When you set out to tell a story, count on this emotion, this fire, this muse within you.

The First Story: "Peekaboo"

"Peekaboo" may be the first homemade story children understand. It's all about primal emotion. The baby — who is utterly dependent on the appearance and disappearance of the caretaker and often anxious that he or she is going to be left there in the crib forever — is entranced by the comic manner in which this feeling is addressed in the little miming story. "Peekaboo" is based on the baby's joy and fear, the "Now I see you, now I don't" aspect of bedtime or naptime. "Peekaboo" is just like real life to the baby, but the time interval is (what a relief!) wondrously, hilariously short. And "Peekaboo" has a happy ending. There's that face again, and this time it stays.

From "Peekaboo" on, the uses of emotion multiply in storytelling. Multiply? That's small potatoes. The uses are squared, cubed, made infinite. The combinations of emotion your child experiences by the age of two are beyond enumeration. Your emotion and your child's emotion together encompass a huge terrain. Use it. When your child has an emotional experience — loses a treasure or is awed by a balloon or a baboon and

doesn't really know all there is to know about it —
give it a story. Take it for material and add your own
touches to it, add to it from your own emotion.

As you do so, your child will feel more understood
by you and feel more willing to accept this whole ar-
rangement of who is going to push the stroller and who
is going to ride in it, who is going to plug in the electric
fan, who is going to pick up the toys, and who is going
to have the authority to discipline and make rules.
(Equal emotions does not mean parents and children
are *entirely* equal. Children need the loving, protective
boundaries of authority. As the psychologist Dr. Lee
Hausner says, "You are not a tall pal.") A child whose
mother and father acknowledge real emotions — name
them, share them, understand them, respect them —
is going to feel loved and worthy, even if there is a
dispute going on, even if it is bedtime. Perhaps, if you
get into the habit of telling stories that explain emotions, the child will even look forward to bedtime.

*Once upon a time there was a little boy who hated
to go to bed. He didn't mind the pajamas with the little
blue and red planes on them, they were nice and warm
on his skin. He didn't mind the feel of his pillow, it
was soft and familiar when he pushed his cheek into
it. What bothered him enormously was that he had to
go to bed and no one else did!*

Memory's Embers

Remembering your past is a vital part of being a storyteller. It is the little hook that will lower you down
to your child on silver cords of meaning. You'll swing

there, I promise, most beautifully as you tell a tale, because memory lights up that huge place in you where meaning is stored. Mine it. Pull it up close again and see this muse glow.

As your child experiences something, try to remember parallel, harmonious incidents from your childhood. Remember the feeling, remember the senses, the color, shape, shadows, and texture of the past. Not only will your memories give you new insights on your own life with this child, but they will help you tell wham-bang stories, stories your child will remember because they have some depth of field and some connected, meaningful, long-range content. You might try to remember the feel of Jergens lotion on a sunburn, the tingly, moist smell of lily of the valley in a neighbor lady's yard, the beautiful color of your mother's eyes, the sound of your father's laugh or how it felt when he boosted you out of the water and tossed you with a wonderful splash into a wave. Whatever you recall, you will begin to feel again what mattered deeply to you as a child.

Having a child has already triggered fresh memories in you. Amazing how you sound just like your mother sometimes or make a gesture exactly like your father's. But more than passively incorporating someone else's tone or gesture, try to consciously welcome, invite, inveigle, coax the inspiration of your memory to stand beside you as you begin to make up stories.

In the great scheme of things, we parents are fortunate to reexperience our childhoods through our young. We all hope to improve upon our parents, even the best of them, to honor their good deeds with our own and not repeat the mistakes they inflicted upon us. Sometimes we sweetly, gratefully remember a wise parental response we now realize was just right, something to admire, to perpetuate for our own children. Other times we sadly or furiously recall some tactic we have decided was inappropriate or worse. When we remember a parallel experience from the past — what it meant then, how it felt — we can add our present wisdom to it, making it all the more profound and valuable. How did you want your parents to respond, long ago? How should they have spoken? What did their eyes reveal in that faraway, related moment? This remembering will help you put your memories to creative use today, give deeper meaning and dignity to them, and enrich a similar experience for your child.

Another thing about memory is that it brings up coincidental, insignificant moments too. Inexplicably, your child's resistance to bedtime triggers in you, say, a memory of yourself, lying in a very dark room and looking down the hall to where your mother stood in silhouette, quietly folding a towel, as though she was waiting for something. Don't dissect it. Just use it; it is an ember for your story. Use how you remember your mother then, how you felt. Why was she waiting there? Why didn't she come back? What was so important about that towel, compared to you? Trust your little, whimsical, wistful associations. They enrich the conscious mind, but more than that, they give you great heaps of material to work with. Memory gives detail, color, zap to the mental idea, and suddenly your story about a little boy who didn't want to go to bed has a remembered object, an inspiration, the towel. The story evolves into something radiant and discovering because you have put a part of yourself into it.

The feeling of bedtime is what you want to explore. Relate to your child's emotion with your own memories and then just jump in.

In his dark room, alone in his airplane pajamas, with only the hall light on, he saw his mother walking away, and he hated it. She stopped for a moment, and his heart rose in hope. But no, she was not coming back, she was only taking up the towel on the floor, the one he'd dropped after the bath. He watched forlornly as she tossed it — blue and yellow stripes — over a doorknob. He began to wonder if that towel was as lonely as he was, hanging there on the knob, dropped by his mother, watching his mother — like he was — as she went down the stairs, thump, thump, thump.

The Lamp of Empathy

What you accomplish with *that* connection — the memory-emotion linkage — is the other human, storytelling triumph: empathy. Empathy is the first-born child of emotion and memory. It's a third party. It does something more than its parents can alone.

Like a lamp, empathy is a domesticated, chosen, plugged-in thing. It throws a very particular light. It is aimed, local, wired to something. It is connected from within you to something outside of you — to another. It is a compassionate light.

When you choose to remember exactly how you really, truly felt about a situation long ago, and then stand up and consider what you've recalled from the higher ground of being a parent looking down on a child who is going through the same moment, what happens is empathy. You remember and feel, but from within another's perspective. You take a leap over the young head, an adult leap that helps you understand what's going on down there.

Empathy, feeling with your child, is a huge fund of inspiration to the storyteller. Put yourself in your child's shoes. Remember in harmony with your child's emotion. Acknowledge it. When you do this, your child realizes he or she is not alone. It is a terrible affliction, at any age, to think, "I'm the only one who has ever felt like this." Your story will assure your child that others have had similar feelings and imply strongly that one such other is *you.* If you imagine the world from your child's perspective from time to time, you will be a better parent and storyteller; you will also have a happier, more secure child. Children, like all of us, deeply, sincerely, profoundly, intensely desire to be understood.

So, sort through your own memories and thoughts until you come to the inner experiences of your own childhood and relate what you get to your current role as a parent. See things, feel things that affect your child by way of your own memories, by identifying with your child. Place yourself in your child's shoes in order to understand and appreciate why your child is charmed by a handful of mud, is intent upon some unacceptable behavior, or is distressed by some "silly" episode in the day. You can use *any* of it in a story. Your empathy will illuminate and guide your characters on their adventures.

If you remember how fresh your legs felt when you ran across a wide field, how you enjoyed your body's

motion, you will stay a few more minutes at the playground watching your child do the same thing, and
perhaps use its airy, wiry, muscular expansiveness in a
story. If you remember the tenderness you felt toward
your treasures as a child, the bag of jacks, your first
watch, your dog's ears, you will treat your child's treasures with more regard, and perhaps give them symbolic prominence and dignity in a tale. If you remember the delightful snap of the ball hitting your mitt,
you'll not only play more catch, but tell stories that
whir and whack with the thrill of the game. If you
remember when you were feverishly sick, how the
walls wobbled with your own nausea, the sickening
sound of the flushing rain outside, you will be a better
healer and have some good material with which to light
up your young patient's life. If you remember the
whoop of accomplishment you felt when you learned
to read, when it happens to your child you will share
the joy and certainly find the subject worthy of a story.
(What was the first word you got? Mine was "look.")
The capacity of being pleased, of being fresh, of being
there with your child — empathetically — is the stuff
of poetry, art, and hundreds, thousands, of stories.

When you are about to tell a story, turn on this
connected, plugged-in lamp inside you. You will find
that empathy comes to the rescue. As empathy imaginatively enters the "I Hate Bedtime" story, it deflects
or allays the child's fears about being left alone by
showing two things you know for sure: one, that the
child's emotion is valuable, even if aimed in the wrong
direction, and two, that there are things that can be
done to allay that feeling, things your child can do,
things you remember doing.

Relive that awful bedtime feeling and remember how or why it went away in you. What did you do, years ago? What happened to soften that sense of self-pity, loneliness, defeat or separation or whatever it was? Remember a remedy that worked for you and offer it imaginatively to your child in a story that ends with what you already confidently know: your child will go to bed and fall asleep.

The boy lay there in the dark and spoke to the towel in a whisper.

"Mom says I'm tired, and I'm definitely <u>not</u>. I hate bedtime. Everybody else gets to do fun things, and I just have to lie here and do nothing."

To his surprise, the towel mumbled something and seemed to sigh.

"What?" said the boy.

"I said, 'I'm pooped,' " said the towel. "I'm glad my work is done today. I'm tired. Your bath was fun for me, but all that drying! Hair, shoulders, legs, feet . . . whew. I'm glad to relax. I've earned this knob. I'm not a bit sorry to be left here. I was afraid your mother was going to take me to the washing machine."

Hunch: Spontaneous Combustion

Somebody said, "Intuition is reason in a hurry." Makes sense to me. However, intuition has gotten a rather bad name in this age of proofs and evidence, especially for women, who are sometimes "accused" of relying on intuition rather than reason. Somehow a fire that ignites by spontaneous combustion is supposed to be more suspect than a fire deliberately lit with a match. Well, a fire is a fire in my book. And a hunch is as good as an encyclopedia when it comes to bedtime stories. Anyone doing quality work — artists, parents, scientists, lawyers, scholars — has to have a good deal of intuition, has to use hunches, has to fly by the seat of the pants.

In storytelling, intuition is often the fastest way to a solution in your story; certainly it is the most inventive and free. When you are about to make up a story, with no planning whatsoever, you absolutely *have* to count on your intuition. It's pragmatic, and pragmatism is something business people are quick to honor, so go ahead. There isn't time to look up your hunch. If you *did* go through books for hours, you would probably find plenty of documentation to back up the reaction you had in the first place. So why bother? Trust your hunch; it's good enough for one story.

If you have a hunch about what is really bothering your child, go with it. Your gut reaction may be the golden ring, the shining gem in the grass that helps solve the problem for your child or for your story. As you work with your hunch in the story, you will improve and aim it simply by going out from it, like an open door, by going through it and moving on.

The boy thought about that for a minute. He would rather not be in the washing machine either. Sloshing and sloshing. Or with his mother, who tended to be ornery doing laundry at night. It was nicer to be in the bed.

The towel said, "She is doing wash, you know. That's what she's doing right this minute. And it's very boring, I can tell you."

"*This* is boring!" said the boy, angrily. "Being *here* is boring," and he punched his pillow with his fist.

"Oh," said the towel with a sigh, "I'd much rather be here. Now's the time for me to think about stuff. Interesting, nice things, like the cotton fields I came from, the wonderful sunshine, the glorious day when I was woven into a towel and made all these pretty colors. Dandelion and blueberry. Boy, that was a day! I like remembering the good things that have happened to me lately. Like coming to your house and belonging to you."

The Starlight of Ancestral Memory

Carl Jung wrote about what he termed the collective unconscious. His concept, as I understand it, was that we are all born with a kind of ancestral memory, a great pool of awareness about human life. In our dreams we see meaningful symbols that are similar from one generation to the next, symbols that express eternal truths about the life experience of the entire human race over many thousands of years. Ancestral memory, according to Jung, is the foundation of what the ancients called "the sympathy of all things."

As a storyteller, I've found that it doesn't hurt to believe this. It gives you confidence that somewhere inside you are voices of your ancestors suggesting one path or another, one vision or another. Their voices are as faint as starlight, as mysterious and distant in the black nothingness, but they are there if you listen very hard and don't expect them to sound just like your grandmother. Their voices are rather like the cumulative whispers and breathing of eons of grandparents. I think you can use this particular muse of ancestral memory in specific detail, if such things come to you, or simply as a confidence builder, letting it reinforce your willingness to go with a hunch.

Indeed, you truly do come from a long and gifted lineage of storytellers. We have a vast oral tradition. Every culture has created tales to amuse people and to explain the world. The Bible, Greek myths, the legends of the Native Americans, fairy tales, nursery rhymes, and lullabies are for the most part anonymous brilliance, stories people made up, repeated, and remembered. I suspect most of this ancestral tale-telling took place in the evening when the family and the mind went inward, when the close of day brought contemplation and close relationships. When you realize that all the great fairy tales were probably told by illiterate people, that the great tales are almost entirely about emotion and memory and the ways to succeed in life, that the great tales are full of images, dreamlike images that stand for human predicaments and hopes, it will give fuel to your fire. Storytelling is an ancient tradition that values the child's difficulties and innocence, values the child in all of us, and attempts to explain, accept, and direct life forward.

"Do you really like it here?" the boy asked.

"Of course!" declared the towel with a huff. "Who wouldn't? I have a nice warm room, a home, my own rack. I've had a pretty good day, too, hanging around. And it ended so happily, thanks to you. I can look forward to tomorrow. I bet you'll get dirty again, won't you? Please?"

"I suppose so . . ." the boy said as he yawned.

"Good," said the towel. "Get your hands dirty, I like to dry your hands. Now, tell me about some nice things that happened to you today. That's the way I go to sleep, thinking about nice things."

"Well, I liked the swings, I liked the way the oatmeal klopped when Mom cooked it . . . I liked . . ." and the boy yawned and yawned, mumbling about his nice times, thinking about his play and dirty hands, and soon, yes, sooner than he thought, he was drifting toward his quiet dreams, easy breathing, and a long, good night's sleep.

Now, this illustrative bedtime story comes from my desire to teach you, as well as from my muses and hunches about my particular children. You, ultimately, would create an entirely different "I Hate Bedtime" story, and that's as it should be. *You* are the key to your own stories. Your emotions, your thoughts, and your inklings about your child are the best guides you could possibly have to making the right story.

You really can count on your five inner muses: emotion, memory, empathy, hunch, and the dreamy light of ancestral memory. Fall into their arms! Great ideas will come to you from a thousand directions, from daily life, and from the past. Having read about them, your creative wings are beginning to flutter, whether you know it or not, and now you are ready for the wider world of imagination, the Big Backyard.

◆ What is now proved was once only imagined.
   — *William Blake*

◆ The most beautiful thing we can experience is the
   mysterious. It is the source of all true art and science.
   — *Albert Einstein*

4

Imagination, the Cat, and the Storyteller: Finding Your Imagination and Using It

◆ ◆ JUST NOW, as I was worrying about how I was going to write about imagination, I decided I needed a cup of coffee — a forgivable delay tactic when facing such a hefty subject. I crossed the yard from my garage studio to the kitchen, poured the coffee, doctored it, and fiddled around. I wondered about imagination for a second or so. As I was returning slowly across the grass, aware that my remaining delay time was getting shorter with every step, I saw a beautiful, smooth black cat, a white diamond on its chest, sitting against a tree in a patch of morning sun. A foreigner. I stood still, holding my cup of coffee; the cat and I exchanged a long, gentle look. When she blinked sleepily, I called quietly to her, hoping this glossy beauty would come to me and let me touch her dense black fur. Hoping, I suppose, for another delay. She stayed still, soft yellow eyes, velvet face, ears perked. "I'll go to her," I thought. But as soon as I took one step, her eyes instantly darkened and she slunk away, unexpectedly skinny, dusty, shrewd-looking, and mean.

She reminded me of what imagination is like. If you quietly look at it, making no move to interrupt it, making no demands — just admiring — it stays put, blinking peacefully, as mysterious, beautiful, and desirable as that cat. But when you try to catch it, pin it down, make it do what you want, it changes into something else entirely and disappears.

You cannot think about your imagination and use it at the same time. Imagination is pulverized by the mental gears that must be shifted in the effort to assess it. You cannot interrupt it. You *can* learn to detect it, however, and bring it out in yourself and remember it. But when it is sitting under your tree, just let it be, stand still and watch.

When you are engrossed in a story and a fine idea comes, you must not stop to analyze where the inspiration came from; rather, you must go with it entirely. When your imagination surfaces, you cannot think of observing its habits without endangering the very idea you have been seeking. You can't stop to be grateful it has arrived; even that kills it. Don't try to fly on an eagle's back and measure its wingspan at the same time. The dream is interrupted by the rational mind.

In the same way, you cannot *will* your imagination, you cannot command it to come with your rational faculties. Gritting your teeth and insisting upon its arrival make that impossible, because you use reason to insist and beg, and reason is an interruption to imagination. Again I say, you cannot think about your imagination and use it at the same time.

The quiet imaginative mood is also incompatible with the noisy, hot grip of adrenalin. Imagination is demolished by immediate fear. If the smoke alarm goes off while you are telling a story, you lose the story until your agitation subsides.

Emotions other than immediate fear and anxiety, however, can be used in combination with imagination and will not interrupt it. In fact, remembered emotion will deeply feed imagination. Think of imagination as a serene force, like a deity or a hawk, sitting high upon a mountaintop, watching and reflecting on the panorama below, observing the thoughts, actions, and emotions of life, the sweep of the landscape. Because imagination is so high up, it can offer insight, perspective, and decent answers to serious dilemmas. Imagination is a way to see and understand emotion better, whether it is grief, disappointment, elation, contentment, or love. Imagination works beautifully with emotion seen from a distance. Wordsworth put it succinctly in his famous dictum on poetry, but the idea applies to imagination too. "Poetry is the spontaneous overflow of powerful feelings: it takes its origin from emotion recollected in tranquillity."

Lightning Bolts and Quiet Whispers

It has taken me long years to understand how imagination comes to people. Mark Twain wrote, "Thunder is good, thunder is impressive; but it is lightning that does the work." That may apply to the creation of the first amoeba in the sea, to trees felled in the night, to forest fires, but not to imagination. A great many of us presume that there has to be something akin to drama and flash to signal something important happening in our thoughts. Subtle visitations by imagination go unacknowledged because we are expecting the lightning bolt of inspiration, the launch of mental transcendence. It doesn't happen.

Imagination is not a blast from on high, it is a whisper in an ordinary room. You have to be quiet to hear it. You have to be patient. You have to be very modest and plain. You have to give up all the egotistical exercise of trying to be inspired and grand. All that *trying* scares it off. All that *wanting* makes it hide. Wanting and trying are the sheet music to imagination, but to hear imagination in action, you have to just let go of worrying about it and play it by ear. You can't hurry it. You can't control it by will power, because duty and inspiration don't mix. Big, shining ideas do not come from strenuous exercise. Imagination is not like thinner thighs.

Testing the Waters

If you want to detect imagination in yourself, to find out that indeed you still have *plenty* of it, you must put on a kind of childish humility. Spend some time not doing "important" things, not achieving, not prizing your can-do. Sit by a window and watch something small and natural, the swaying of a branch, the light on a brick wall, the clouds. You have to "go fishing," or take a long, pointless, wandering walk from time to time. You have to muse. When you are quietly strolling along, in no rush, just looking around — watching the dogs run in the park, noticing a weed sprouting by a fence — slowly some imaginative thought surfaces. Unexpected, interesting, easy-arriving. Small, mundane observations can lead to a chain reaction of thoughts, all of which, no matter how disconnected or seemingly trivial, are the stuff of imagination.

A few days ago, for example, after a drizzle of rain, I was walking in the park, watching the grassy, pebbly ground pass beneath my feet. It wasn't an engrossing sight, so I closed my eyes for a moment, still walking, and was struck by the very specific sweet smell of wet grass in the air. I opened my eyes and thought, no, not grass, that green smell is probably the smell of wet roots. I began to muse about how to describe the powerful fragrance, whatever its source. I kept reverting to the idea that it just smelled green, but I knew that didn't really make sense, green is not a smell. My imagination clicked in, unnoticed. I started to play with the idea, senseless or not: if a smell can be green, what does blue smell like, or red, or yellow? In my chain reaction of thoughts, I came to the phrase "blue as a lake" and assigned a sand and wave smell to blue. "Red as a tomato," which my mother adores and puts pepper on, so red smells peppery to me. "Yellow as a lemon," and that was just right. I decided black has no scent at all because it is so closed-in and airless, nor does white, which is the purest of airs. What's the point? Nothing less than my certain knowledge that my imagination was engaged for a few minutes there and was refreshed by this series of trivial thoughts. I could have taken any one of them and turned it into a bedtime story. Or piled them all together and made a tale about the only rainbow in the world that arched a bouquet of fragrance over one little town, and what that did to all the people there.

Imagination can come during strenuous exercise, when your blood is pumping and your mind is adrift. Strange, wonderful thoughts happen on the jogging path, half a mile in, or when you're doing the stair machine at the health club, or laps in the pool. Pay attention to the fleeting blips of thought that come as your heart pounds, as you sweat.

Inactivity can lead to inspiration, too. The famous stories about scientific discoveries may be apocryphal, but they teach an important lesson about imagination. Newton was sitting under an apple tree when one fell on him and he "discovered" gravity. Fulton was in the kitchen watching the teapot come to a boil, idly watching the lid wobble, when suddenly he came up with the idea of the steam engine. While climbing into the bath, Archimedes was struck by the idea that he could measure weight by the amount of water the object displaced. He supposedly ran naked through the streets shouting "Eureka!" Now, I ask you. Were they trying? Not at the time. Yes, they had strived and searched for an answer perhaps for weeks or years, but it didn't come until their minds were engrossed in something mundane. The inspiration came after all the trying was over, when they were relaxed in an ordinary moment.

I sometimes wonder if my best mothering moments have not been in my little bemused stories, those times when I stopped trying to be somebody big, important, in charge, capable, and on time. I try so hard to be a fine mother, to use my heart and wits, make good decisions, laugh off frustrations. But when I just sink down in the relaxed air of a small story, on a rumpled bed, away from the real world of mothering, I wonder if in this mode I am perhaps at my most profound, most loving, and most inspired. My husband would dispute it, and I'd be glad if he did. ("My wife's not much of a mother, but she tells a *hell* of a bedtime story" wouldn't please me enormously.) And, who knows, my children might praise instead my "inspired" spaghetti sauce. (Straight from a jar.) But deep down, I still wonder if my most shining moments of mothering, in which I tell my children most effectively how much I love them and believe in them, haven't in fact been in some bedtime yarn about a hang-gliding ladybug or a woman made all of dreams or a boy who took a mouse in his pocket to the Statue of Liberty.

Imagination Lives in the Present Tense

The difference between imagination and all its relatives
— wishing, worrying, planning, hoping — is that
imagination is something that happens in and around
the present. As the writer Brenda Ueland says in her
book *If You Want to Write,* imagination takes place in
a mode of thought that is entirely "in the present,"
not reflecting, not projecting, but resting entirely,
slowly, almost imperceptibly, in the present moment.
Imagination pipes up at odd times: when you are waiting for the person you called to answer the phone,
when you are filling your ears with water in the
shower, when you are waiting for the green light in
traffic, or while you are sitting by a river doing nothing, just looking. It comes during "dead time." Don't
dismiss it, welcome it. When it happens, write it down,
or just make a mental note. Even if you don't manage
these mental notes frequently at first, you will in a
week or two. It's like remembering your dreams. If
you *want* to remember your dreams and make an effort to do so, you will. And by the way, dreams can
provide you with more story material. Listen to them;
they are messages from your imagination.

The creative impulse comes from following your
nose. It sees, it feels, it quietly hears *now*, in the present. It comes when you wonder about something, not
in an assessing, intellectual way but in the way of a
child. When you are absorbed in the present moment,
observing something without expectations, when you
let your mind wander with its shoes off, barefoot,
that's when imagination speaks.

Children are so imaginative, I think, because they live so much of the time in the present. They are not worrying about the past and future things we worry about. They don't have nervous thoughts like, Did I unplug the circle saw? Will there be enough money in the checking account for these groceries? What if this airplane has too much weight for takeoff? They just pay attention to what is happening right then, watching for anything with peaceful interest.

You must try to spend some time in this mode. It will give your imagination time to surface, space to grow, and give you a chance to recognize it. Be still for a few minutes a day. Allow a slow collection of thoughts to come. Meditate, walk, weed the garden, do something mindless, live in the moment. If you have to, put time for this mode on your calendar. Swim back and forth and listen to the water plunk as your hand hits it, feel the coolness slide through your fingers, see the waves you make. Be sensuous. Turn off the mental jets. Let some sound repeat while you do nothing; lie on the laundry room floor and listen to the thump of the *dryer*, I don't care. Go to the stairwell at the office where no one comes, and sit there, alone. Let your mind relax. Feel the hardness of the step, study the color of the paint on the walls, smell the railing, get to your senses: nose, eye, hand, ear. Count your heartbeats, take long breaths, just *be*.

Let your imagination go outside, inside, wherever it wants to. It is the child within you. When you let it wander, and softly, attentively stay close by, your imagination will lead you to wonderful places.

As you go into this kind of dreaming present, keep delight at your side, keep a quiet willingness to be

pleased with whatever comes to you. To paraphrase
Alan McGlashan in his book *The Savage and Beautiful
Country*, as you inwardly smile at your own thoughts,
as you stop willing and criticizing them, you will create
an inner stillness in which glimpses of things and ideas
too fleeting and tangential, too wayward and fugitive
for ordinary life, can delicately come home to you.
These thoughts have been wandering like Hansel and
Gretel in the human mind for centuries. Your imaginative thoughts are, in McGlashan's words, the "long-
lost children" of the human race. Open the door and
take them in. Love them and watch over them; they
are so young and have been so neglected in our society.
Try to listen to what they say, learn their language,
see their pictures, bend to them, they can teach you.
And they, like your own children, will show you an
amazingly open space, a beautiful new landscape, full
of shining grasses and tiny blue flowers. (Or do you
like yellow? Yellow it is!) These long-lost children of
your imagination will take your hand and bring you to
a state of mind where life is beginning, where the sun
is rising redly, where the air is divine and your inner
voices sing.

Making the Big Move:
Putting Your Imagination to Work

Now that you've had some time to get in touch with
your imagination, to recognize its brief or beguiling
visits during your day, I want to tell you how to put
your imaginative powers to use.

The Inner Room

When you start to tell stories, trust that your imagination is there in you, in the background. Be alert and relaxed. Don't try to catch or force your imagination, just wait. Think — lovingly — how can I give shape to this, what can I use to tell this story? Quietly, I think, a small door will open in your mind, leading into a glassy room of imagination, bright and cluttered with sensations, memories, and the images of your life and perhaps the lives of others. In this room is everything you will need for your stories. No clock ticks, time is forgotten. When you enter this room of the imagination, something in you — a quiet whisper — will select an appropriate snippet from the clutter. Usually your selection will be unthought. There's a "granted" quality to the thing you choose; your imagination will go right to the picture of something that is right for your story. It may be as mundane as a handful of rubber bands, it may be as majestic as the Rockies, it may be as odd as an island of zebras. You probably won't know just how you are going to use the particular image, but trust that it is instinctively right, and that as the story emerges, it will become clearer. Breathe. Listen to yourself.

The Imaginative Voices of the Storyteller

There are really two kinds of inner voices. One is the sound and chatter of an ambitious, efficient, capable, scheduled, do-it person, yelling "Faster faster, more more" at you all the time, your get-through-the-day voice. The other is the deeper, more resonant and pro-found voice of the spirit that comes from quiet, con-templative stillness and peace. You will be relieved to know that I believe either voice is sufficient to the needs of the beginning storyteller.

Let's start with the one you have in spades right now, the surface voice, the closest one. This voice is loaded with material! As you try to get rolling imagi-natively, this voice will begin to seek an appropriate two or three things from the clutter of the day for you to choose from.

Let's say the event you want to discuss with your son is the fun he had this afternoon when you made hard-boiled eggs and handed him the slicer. How he had enjoyed it, fitting the peeled egg into the little curve, pulling down the harplike wires, cutting the egg into ten perfect slivers, and eating them with gusto. Your surface-imaginative voice will, for instance, sug-gest that you tell the story from the egg's point of view, but you discard that because it seems painful. Next, your surface voice suggests that you make the story about a chicken that wanted to lay a hard-boiled egg. But that seems tricky. So you muse a bit and your voice says, well, how about a story about a cat with ten kittens who wanted to make one egg go equally all around. Now you can get going. Hand the slicer to one of the kittens at the end of the tale and you've got a good one, one your child will enjoy.

Or let's say the issue is the haircut this past after-noon. It was four o'clock, your child was tired, so was the barber. Your first voice will tell you that you should have made the appointment for ten in the morning. But that's not much of a story. Next comes the idea that the person getting a haircut was not your child but a cricket. That sounds interesting. How to cut a cricket's hair? (Don't be so literal as to say, "But crickets don't have hair" — go with it.) Your busy, top-of-the-head voice may suggest some very small scissors. Almost invisible? Made of glass? Made of silver? Are they magic? This could make a haircut fun. You are on your way with a story.

Your surface voice, you see, is absolutely loaded with material. Your head is spinning with it. Now let me tell you the other good news. As you practice and experiment with this nearly endless first imaginative voice, the other, the *second* voice of the storyteller will begin to emerge.

This quiet, serene, solitary voice is absolutely the grander one, the one that brings up the greatest, biggest fish, the one that is attached to the universe somehow. The profound universal voice will begin to come to you after you begin a habit, a routine if you will, of storytelling. I cannot emphasize this strongly enough. Those few minutes of quiet repose with your child, that period of tender dreaminess, those left-field excursions you invent, will begin to add up, as though you *had* had time to take a regular hour's walk or pause with just your senses somewhere away from the crowd. Those gathered minutes will begin to accrue as reflective and pure thought. Over time, your stories will tap the deep places that meditation, contemplation, or prayer reaches. Each five or fifteen minutes you spend telling a story will begin to fill that second, deep, inner voice of yours.

Your imagination is so resilient that after only a couple of weeks of storytelling, you'll begin to hear your profound voice, feel the peace you associate with depth, and discover that your imaginative, profound voice is very much alive inside you. Told from this great voice, your story about the egg would become a different tale entirely, more philosophical or all-encompassing. It might deal with the miracle of birth itself, with perfection, with breakthrough, with transformation.

Now You Have It

Remember, all day long your imagination has been storing important things, musings and observations, in your inner room. Subtle moments are gathered there too: when you smelled a gardenia and thought of your sister, when you heard a squeak and for an instant saw a porch swing from the past, when you heard a melody and envisioned a loved one no longer near — it's all there within you. Your inner room holds the relaxed thoughts, the flashes of intuition, and moments of "being" that go unspoken all day long.

Decide to live in the present for the duration of a story and don't think about imagination while you're using it. Know that imagination feeds on emotion recollected in tranquillity. As you set out to tell stories, trust your busy, surface voice of imagination — it is vast, clever, and amusing. As stories accumulate and time goes by, the profound voice will come to you. As Faulkner said, "Listen to the voices."

Now, As for Your Excuses . . .

"I'm no Charles Dickens."

Perhaps the main difference between us — not to last past the end of this chapter, I hope — is that I have come to know I have a fine imagination, while you may still be struggling with such last-minute excuses as "I'm no Charles Dickens, I can't do it."

The stories and rumors that surround the artistic giants of our civilization can be so intimidating that they stop us in our tracks. In only ten years, Dickens wrote *David Copperfield, Bleak House, Hard Times, Little Dorrit,* and *A Tale of Two Cities.* (With my life, it would take me ten years to *read* them.) Mozart wrote more music than any other composer and died at the age when many of us are just getting out of graduate school. Handel wrote the "Messiah" in twenty-four days. Michelangelo painted perhaps the greatest work of the modern age, the Sistine Ceiling, and considered himself a sculptor. They say Shakespeare never blotted a line.

Who can hope to match them? Some of us are daunted by these stories and let them create an easy out, an excuse to quit trying to be creative. Don't do it. Your imagination may not rank up there with the great, life-affirming artists of the ages, but you do have enough to give your children a sight of you walking, even flying, in their imaginative world. It's not the Sistine Ceiling, but it's off the ground. And think about this — your love for your child is equal to the inspiration of any artistic genius.

"That's a woman's job."

I asked my husband once why he doesn't tell stories, and his answer was "That's a mother's message." Now, I can honestly understand, with me in the house, how he would say that. I've been telling stories for fifteen years, and routines do get set in cement. Yet, much as I love the man, on this one, he's all wet.

Storytelling, imagination, has nothing to do with gender. In fact, fathers and grandfathers have told stories to children for generations. My father did, and did so brilliantly. Although most fathers are more removed from the fray of childraising, they still have the human desire to entertain, instruct, and enjoy their young. What is so fitting about stories, even to fathers who disdain diapering, is that storytelling *is* noble work and highly enjoyable. It's quiet, relaxing, attached, and loving. Shakespeare's soldier-king, Henry V, said, "What infinite heart's ease / Must kings neglect that private men enjoy." I love that phrase, "infinite heart's ease." Fathers need it as much as mothers do. For men or women who have been away from their children all day, the message your story brings is this: now that we are together again, I want to do something special with you, just the two of us. I care about you.

The father's profound voice of imagination is genderless, just as a mother's is. But every individual has unique experiences with which to tell stories. In some families, the father's surface imagination may have fed on different things all day, and his material may be very gender-specific, and *useful* because of that. A man who begins to tell stories may be more inclined to tell a tale inspired by the fishing lures he tied last night or the pickup basketball game he joined after work. My father told me a great one about a cat named Rainbow who got into the shaving cream. All fine story material. And how about ties? Or suspenders — they'd be a snap in a story! My point is, men and women are equal in their stores of valuable experience to be given to a child.

So I urge you all, male and female alike, to leap into this wonderful form of communication. Imaginative stories and the messages they carry to children have absolutely nothing to do with gender roles and everything to do with enhancing your child's inner well-being.

"I don't know where my story should go."

In the litany of excuses, this is a common one. Perhaps you're worried that you can't tell a story that will speak to your child's concerns because you don't have all the answers. Well, join the club. Nobody knows "the" answers, just *some* of them, *some* of the time. Life itself is an imaginative search for answers, with the same old questions repeating themselves. So, please don't think you have to have life all figured out in order to tell a little tale and fool around with your imagination. "The best lack all conviction, while the worst / Are full of passionate intensity," wrote Yeats. Give yourself permission to be a bit at sea in this world. Perhaps your doubt puts you among the best. History is full of wonderful doubters.

But history is another potential source of imagination-bashing. Because written history is squashed into so few minutes of reading compared with the time it took to happen, it makes people in the past seem as though they knew where they were going; no great figure in a history book is seen to putter, page after page. Not many imaginative forays have been included in the historical record. Yes, we have alchemy to laugh at, we have the Fountain of Youth nowhere in Florida, but that's about it. And history seems to assign people missions that they didn't have, or didn't know they had, at the time. As the science writer Timothy Ferris maintains, there is no evidence that Einstein ever got up in the morning with the intention of theorizing on the expansion of the universe. He plugged along, just as we do.

So, to make a great discovery or create something that will lead the human race forward, we don't *have* to know where we are going. In the same way, on a smaller scale, you have no way of knowing if your imaginative story might not just make a superb, lasting, formative, valuable impression on your developing child.

There is a persistence of mystery in imagination that involves each of us. Learning to love the eternal questions is part of the knack, perhaps *the* consoling gambit, of living out a lifetime. So, resign yourself to the fact that every time you start a story, you will begin the search for an answer, and that search will present an astounding map of roads to choose from. Discovering the end of the story, by way of your imagination, is half the fun. In fact, this search for the answer is actually a wonderful *subject* for a story.

Once upon a time there was a young girl who loved sparklers because she could write in the air with them.

She loved how the starry white line hung there, em-blazoning the night with her word, whatever word she felt like. One night, on the Fourth of July, she wrote "The Answer" over and over again till her arm ached and her eyes were dazzled. The next morning, she went out to see what remained. The sparklers sat in a jar of water, like a black bouquet. But the sun had filled the yard, and a breeze was leaning over the grass, and way up there in the blue was a high-flying bird trailing one long piece of something. It was probably just a string.

I can tell you from experience, you *can* get there even if you don't know the answers, the destination. Imagination does not *have* a destination, and that is what makes it so exciting to work with. You are not on someone else's track, you are free to cross the continent in an instant, if you want to, on the force of your own invention. Imagination is a force inside you that helps you *discover* a destination, one that is particularly appropriate for you and for your child.

"What if I get stuck in the middle of a story?"

Worrying about your inability to sustain a whole story even if you can come up with an initial idea is understandable but stubbornly misses the *point* of imagination. If you are in the middle of a story and suddenly stop to worry about it, interrupt the flow of imagination with a rational or irrational question, *of course* you will come to a screeching halt. Remember my black cat in the yard. As you are sitting there, suddenly worried, using your mental faculties, imagination bolts! The thinking and worrying and wanting gets in the way; the rational intensity defeats your imagination. As I have said before, thinking about imagination and using it don't mix. While you're working yourself into a snit about your imaginative powers, or lack of them, you are using the very faculty that prevents their reemergence. You become your own worst enemy.

Try this tack. Take the pressure off yourself. This isn't *Hamlet* you're working on, it's a bedtime story. This isn't the play-offs, you're just shooting some hoops. This is a situation akin to missing the toss to the wastebasket with a Kleenex. It is not the end of the world to get stuck. If you don't know where to go, just stay where you are. It's all right. Stand there and dribble and let your imagination catch its breath; no one's going to steal the ball. Bend your knees, pivot a bit, check out the game so far, look around *within* the context of the story, be imaginatively alert. Keep talking about the story, *be* in the story, involved, seeing, attentive to the *story*, and I promise, the rhythmic, soothing dribble will steady you, and your imagination will return and give you an opening, a what-next, a clear shot. Then, as they say, go for it.

So, Don't Be Afraid

You *are* imaginative; you were born with it. If you're out of shape, it may take a week or so to get it back and flexing, which isn't much compared to aerobics. Don't worry about inspired genius; a lot of discovery comes when you least expect it, and poetic frenzy, if there is such a thing, comes from years of stored reflection and musing. Remember that imagination is a force, a quiet force for discovery, that takes place in the present. It is enthusiastic, generous, and open-minded, but don't try to mix reason or adrenalin with it. Feed it with reflection and with your love for your child, and it can be with you every night to help you create beautiful stories.

♦ And this our life, exempt from public haunt,
Finds tongues in trees, books in the running brooks,
Sermons in stones, and good in everything.
— *William Shakespeare*

5

Calling In the Muses: Mood and Environment

♦ ♦ REMEMBER you are not going to plan, strain, and cogitate when you set out on your first story. Relax and let the muses arrive. You are ready to visualize some gentle, simple idea, ready to open the door into that adjacent room of your imagination, look around, and then close it gently when it is time to go. This is a form of relaxation, discovery, and pleasure for you and your child.

This mood arrives more easily if you have a habitual place for storytelling. Settling down to a story again and again in the same place gives the beginner a sort of habit that helps to ease the shyness, gives a whistle to your inspirations, and alerts the child to a kind of special occurrence. You'll begin to associate this place with your inner voice, your imagination, and things will go more easily. Just like the yawn that arrives when your child's head hits the pillow, the environment of your story, the literal place you sit or lie down, triggers the imaginative world within you.

You need to be alone and quiet with the child in a private, cozy place. Clearly, the most practical place is the child's bedroom, and the child should be in bed, teeth brushed, and whatever routines you require completed. The point is, the work is over, there is nothing more to be done after the story but kiss, say good night, and go to sleep. Quiet time with children at bedtime has become a part of our species behavior; we are still in the rhythm of the ages, the rhythms of sun and moon, so, let history do some of the work for you. This is a natural time and place for storytelling.

But lives these days have crazy forms. If there is a better time than bedtime for you, go ahead, do your storytelling in the car on the commute to school, do it on a regular afternoon stroll together, do it during bathtime, whenever. Just try to choose a time that is dependable, cozy, and long enough to let you get rolling; fifteen minutes is usually more than enough. Choose a time when you are not in danger of having to leap up, wave a finger, and say with a sheepish grin, "To be continued . . ." That's not good. It can backfire like mad. The worst backfire is that you won't remember the story you were telling. Almost as serious as a mental blank is the act of leaving your child and your hero in the lurch. Cozy, unhurried time is a key to storytelling. It doesn't really matter where.

Don't allow a visitor to sit in on the storytelling, not at first anyway, perhaps never, but that's up to you. At the start, you don't need to be inhibited by spouses, friends, in-laws. This is not a performance. You are not to worry about the impression you are going to make here or about how some adult is going to see and understand your efforts. You'll clam up.

In this quiet environment, make a comfortable connectedness with your child. Just as you probably do when reading together, be physical: hold hands, snuggle in the rocking chair, lie down or sit on the side of the bed with your child, whatever seems most appropriate to you. The slide of your affectionate fingers along your child's cheek, the feel of that small hand in yours, is tremendously calming and good for both of you. Turn off the radio or the mobile or whatever makes noise and distraction. Dim the lights. Make the room nice for yourselves, warm, comfortable, enclosed, private, and affectionate. The day softens as you lean together.

How to Prepare Yourself

You don't have to plan your story over dinner. That is what this book is about. You don't have to make strategies, preparatory notes, memos; nothing of the organized adult is expected here. Rather, this is the time for you to just kick off your shoes, flop down with your child, sigh, and enjoy the separate peace that children's rooms seem to exude, the innocent, trusting, tender air there, far from the rest of the world. Just take it in for a moment before you begin.

Try to put your mind in that quiet place where imagination can speak to you. Usually, a sigh gets you started. You cannot remain rattled about scattered toys, pajamas, wet heads, dirty fingernails, or any other claptrap. Any previous moments between parent and child where authority and obedience were involved have to be over before you start your story. We are not The Big Boss Telling a Tale. It is very important that you have nothing on your mind to distract you from these next few minutes, nothing pressing for the duration of the story. You can't be thinking about the calls you have to return after bedtime, or the report you have to get out, or anything at all. That is all for later. You have to be taking that easy stroll I talked about. This is the present, and the present is all there is. You need to go at it relaxed and trusting, easy, loose, happy, no rush. After what you've been through to get the child into this bedded position, I am confident the mood will be welcome indeed! Put your feet up; the hard part is over. Now for the fun.

Don't worry about the story. The next chapter will give you a very simple outline of the basic tale. It's so easy, it's amazing. For now, just know that what you say will have slipped into your imaginative room in one of those moments when you were just idly thinking any old thing. What you say will be interesting enough to earn you a heartfelt, happy hug from your little audience. Trust that you will think of something. Whichever rationale you prefer — doing something generous and ancient for your child, or doing something just to relax and explore yourself — here is one of those celestial, dinging, golden moments when both philosophies apply. The Self and Others are about to join in storytelling.

Think of yourself as charged and fortified by a muscular, soaring, vaulting muse, a muse as potent as Beethoven's: your love for your child. Everyone recognizes the need for a muse, even Shakespeare. He called for it at the beginning of *Henry V:*

> O for a Muse of fire, that would ascend
> The brightest heaven of invention;
> A kingdom for a stage, princes to act
> And monarchs to behold the swelling scene!

Now there's an invocation. But if that's too stirring, try a dulcet, soothing tack. There's one more thing you can do, a pretty much guaranteed muse-caller. Think about that time you have known on so many nights before you go to bed, when you come back to check on your sleeping child. It's late, you readjust the covers whether they need it or not; the light is the way your child likes it; the safety and well-being of the moment flood over you; and you lean down to look closely at that person, sleeping. How close to tears you can come sometimes, just looking. You can almost breathe the innocence and purity and promise. The child's unique sleeping position, evolving from infancy, fills you with tenderness. The face in complete repose, the relaxation of the hands, the motionless wonder of those legs, which suddenly seem longer. There is no hurry as you look down. There is nothing but love and an inexpressible feeling of wanting to be worthy of this precious child. Try to retrieve this feeling as you anticipate telling the story; it will bring out the finest in you.

I hope the things I have told you so far will engender a magical self-confidence in you now as you are about to start creating your castles or pillow factories, inventing your scenes, adventures, and heroes. How wonderful if you feel your own wings, a pair of broad, beautiful wings, all shining and strong, folded lightly inside you. You are at that clifflike moment when you are about to spring up and leap off into thin air, with no particular plans of what you are going to see or where you are going to land. I believe you will soar like a bird.

♦ From father I got my bearings, the seriousness in life's pursuits; from mother the enjoyment of life and love of spinning fantasies.
— *Johann Wolfgang von Goethe*

♦ Air, fire, water, and earth I presented to him as beautiful princesses, and everything in all nature took on a deeper meaning. We invented roads between stars, and what great minds we would encounter . . . He devoured me with his eyes . . .
— *Katharine Elizabeth Textor (Goethe's mother)*

6

The Nitty-Gritty: Basic Story Structure

♦ ♦ NO PALAVER, NOW; no more setting the stage and adjusting the lights. You're ready. Here's a quick run-down on what I think is involved in every successful bedtime story. First comes a short prologue, "Once upon a time"; then there are five basic parts:

(1) There was a likable hero
(2) who had reason to set out on a journey
(3) when a threat occurred
(4) from which there was a hero-inspired way out
(5) which resulted in a safe return and a happy ending.

Fairy tales take this form almost without exception. I use fairy tales as models when I make up a story because they are flat-out brilliant patterns for bedtime stories. Why reinvent the wheel? Fairy tales came from people winging it just as you will do. They were made-up stories that were so good they were repeated and refined until the tales became the archetypal sort of cultural memory they are today. The Grimm brothers, after all, just went out and took dictation from the storytellers of Europe. These fairy tales — as your tales will — looked at the puzzlement children feel in the face of experience and told them that to be puzzled or worried is not unique or anything to be ashamed of. Fairy tales — as your tales will — offered solutions to the puzzles and gave children a vicarious experience of victory over problems.

The great long ones add elaboration on one or several of the five parts above, but basically that's all fairy tales are up to, the five basic parts. The simple elegance of these concepts is easy to befriend and put to use.

"Once upon a time" is the accustomed beginning to most fairy tales and stories. It is a good way for you to start too. This familiar device, cousin to "abracadabra," is the incantation that makes the doors to enchantment swing open and the land of fantasy beckon just beyond.

There is a magically uncertain air about "Once upon a time," a poetic quality, a deliberate vagueness. Everyone knows that it is not now, today. It could be past, most likely it *is* past, semantically, but for the purposes of a story it could be the future, too. Most important, it is not here and now. "Once upon a time" places the story outside external reality — places it, as

Bruno Bettelheim says, "in a state of mind — that of the young in spirit."

When you tell a story you want to create a suspension of time. You do not need to use the exact words "Once upon a time," but the impact must be the same. You could say, "Long ago in a land of wishes," "In a far-off kingdom," "Close to a great castle there lived," or "In olden days," if you are drawn to the formalized entrances of fairy tales. Or you could make up your own timeless phrase. Do it if you can, and repeat it as you tell stories so that your child will come to think of it as your very own secret passageway: "Not now, but far away," "Once, once, once, when trees could walk," or whatever pleases you. But make it poetically clear that it is a distant time, a rather forgotten time, a time where your child's imagination can fill in the images. For the story to work on the various levels you wish it to, you cannot start in the mundane reality in which you live. Don't say, "This morning in the busy street I saw a dinosaur . . ." The story is not here, close by, but elsewhere, outside, far away. "Once upon a time" immediately separates you and the child from the realities of time and place, giving memory, according to Coleridge, its imaginative home.

This *distancing* accomplishes several things at once: first of all, you are not going to misinstruct your child about the presence of dinosaurs, witches, et cetera. This story does not lap directly at the child's toes like a horrible, unseen tide. We do not want to worry about finding a tyrannosaurus rex tomorrow at kindergarten. With the device of timelessness you are transported to a place of imagination where you see, as your child does, that today and its tyrannical ways of being doesn't have to apply. Water can misbehave, water can run up the mountain if you want it to, water can talk.

Once upon a time in a beautiful, underwater place where plants could whisper, fishes could speak, and the sea could hold a conversation with you, something quite wonderful happened.

In this land of "once upon a time," you, the story-teller, now have the freedom to move in magical ways; you have the power to invent creatures that can behave as people do, beasts that do not exist, events that could not really happen. As you make this magical leap, you are becoming one with the inner self, one with the imaginative voices, one with the feelings we have inside us. You become the mirror of inner experience.

(1) There was a likable hero

This is probably the crux of everything. The character, the hero of your story, is the focus of it all. I use "hero" as a male and female word, just like "author" or "parent." If you don't have a hero in mind, which at first you may not, ask your child for a suggestion. Most often the young child will suggest an animal that he or she likes, and you are off and running.

Instinctively, I think children choose animal heroes who have qualities the children identify with, creatures in whom they see something of themselves. There is some value in animal stereotypes, as in all stereotypes. With all tolerance, I say that pig means one thing, kitten means another. Pigs have appetites of some repute, but they also happen to be more intelligent than dogs. Eagle is one quality, sparrow another. They are shorthand ways of identifying certain traits. For ease of telling, it makes sense to consider for a moment what your child's "animal of choice" means to him or her. I'll bet the choice will be a small animal, not a lion or a bear. But we are all different in subtle ways and are always changing within, so perhaps one evening your child will want a pterodactyl hero. If so, try to intuit what that creature embodies for your child. Find something of value in it — do not make it the monster in the story — for most often your child is suggesting the hero, not the villain. And perhaps the child's wanting a pterodactyl has to do with wanting to fly and be powerful or frightening to others. This is not an insane desire, it is the product of helplessness or worry, and gives you a marvelous clue, an understanding rope to follow into the cave toward the issue your child is concerned about and the gist of the story your child intuitively desires.

Consider what you know of the animal's nature and use it as the fabric of your story. Quickly think of its natural strengths and weaknesses, its powers and enemies. And then set out on your story. After the "once upon a time" part, spend a minute describing the animal's body and face. Try to imagine how its tail, paws, or ears look, whether its eyes have a nice color or shape. Relate the animal to something the child likes; for instance, you could say the eyes were the color of chocolate, or the fur felt just like the binding on a blanket. Get tactile to start and let your inner voice get rolling. As you begin, give yourself some time to become engrossed. It is not hard to put words of description together, just be honest about it, be truthful.

Perhaps the dog's ears were curly and brown and he had a stripe on his forehead that looked as if ice cream had melted down. As you go on, you will find that details just sort of drift into your mind. Some of them will come from memory, perhaps a dog or cat you knew as a child, or a squirrel you watched one day at the park, or a picture in a book you once read. Let your imagination and memory take you. If you are going to rely on a remembered pet in your childhood, you will be on good ground, because you probably cared about it.

Because caring is what character is all about. If you care about your hero, you will invest its fantasy character with your own affection, and, too, you will gather inspiration from things your child enjoys or admires. If your child likes to draw, give your hero an artistic trait; if your child admires the carpenters redoing the back porch, give your hero a hammer; if your child has been popping bubble wrap that day, perhaps your hero could make a boat out of it. These appealing details go right to your child's heart; for indeed, you want your child to care about the hero too. You want a sympathetic, likable main character in your story. This isn't the place for anti-heroes.

Down in the sea's musical depths, where the fish spoke and the seaweed whispered, lived one of the liveliest creatures in the world. He was a spotted dolphin, and his parents called him Scoot because he was so playful and fast. His whole body was shiny and smooth, almost as blue as the water. His back was dappled with hundreds of milk-colored spots, like a fawn's spots, or a sky thick with stars.

Now, when I said "no anti-heroes" above, that does

not mean the hero has to be *all* good. In fact, mischief has sold millions of books (Beatrix Potter and Maurice Sendak come to mind), and is still quite valid in story-telling. What your child cares about at first is not whether the hero is "good," but whether there is something in the hero's condition that is sympathetic, that makes your child see something of himself or herself in the hero. Don't be explicit about the hero's goodness or badness, as in "Once there was a very naughty bunny in an apartment at 564 Laurel." Rather, try to suggest that the bunny's situation was one your child would sympathize with, as in "Once there was a very lovable bunny who lived in a hole right under a drainspout. Every time it rained, he was flooded. But he was too young to dig a new hole and too small to move the spout." The hero may end up *doing* something naughty, like removing a pail from a sandbox and trying it for a door, but the hero is not innately naughty.

Beatrix Potter has a mouse couple, Hunka and Munka, who invade and trash a dollhouse, smashing miniature plaster hams and lobsters all over the place, taking the feather bolsters back to their children, and there is no real harm done, no one is being denied real food in a dollhouse. My point is, you don't have to browbeat your child with dogmatic stories in which the hero has absolutely civilized behavior at all times. Let your children know that there is a place for misbehavior in the world, a place for muddy shoes, a time for dawdling, and your stories will be better.

When Scoot played hide-and-seek with friends, his spots would sometimes look just like bubbles and no one could find him. He loved games, but his favorite sport was not hiding, it was what he called "tummy-riding." He loved to follow the whale-watching boat and ride on the high white wave by its side. He got a kick out of seeing all the people run to the railings with cameras and binoculars. He always smiled and waved a flipper.

Trickster stories take mischief a bit farther. The hero is a sort of Robin Hood type, stealing or doing wrong for a higher purpose. You may enjoy telling them. A trickster story probably best comes from a witty storyteller, but even if you are not Woody Allen you could pull it off. Tricksters, in oral tradition, steal the secrets of the gods. Prometheus stole fire from Mount Olympus and brought it to earth, and that theft, given the need for fire in human life, was a theft worth doing, but he paid for it with a near eternity of suffering. The trickster in Native American mythology steals wind, rain, or snow to bring order into the cosmos. The fox in Grimm's "The Golden Bird" advises the hero to steal the golden bird in the wooden cage, and this theft results at last in justice and happiness for all the characters. The boy in Grimm's "The White Snake" steals a bite of the king's forbidden dinner, but in so doing he understands the language of animals. It is on a different order than stealing a radio to buy drugs. It is on a different order than having your characters steal things selfishly. You have to ask, when is it all right, in my judgment, to steal? Perhaps you do not want stories about theft whatsoever.

Now, while I say that mischief or wave-riding is occasionally welcome, and that goodness versus badness is not the issue around which your child identifies with the hero, I want to also say that your hero should know right from wrong. While the child's attraction to the hero may not be because he is "good," the hero, in your hands, should know the meaning of the word. The very definition of hero, according to the historian Barbara Tuchman and the dictionary, implies a nobility of purpose. The hero must have some form of higher purpose in life. Originally, heroes were half mortal, half divine, and expressed the value systems, the ethics, of the nations that created them.

Your hero should not be an intellectual anti-hero, a pop-culture creature who gets away with thefts, abuse of others, murder and mayhem. I think it is important for you as a parent to use your stories to reflect what you believe to be right and wrong, perhaps to reflect the ethical, historical opinion as well. (I'll talk more about values in the next chapter.) Your child has to grow up in this society, and has to hope to improve it somehow, not just survive in it. So, I caution you not to be too quick to weave into your stories the latest media-driven revision of right and wrong. Mature, protective, parental prudence requires reflection and consideration on history's great human values before you use fantasy to deliver a diatribe to your child on some new, raw opinion you might have come up with this morning from reading the newspaper. I also urge you not to get into telling stories that dwell on victimization of children. Domestic violence, while not absent in fairy tales, is always sketched extremely vaguely, primarily as deprivation or servitude, a kind of situational shorthand for juvenile stages of life as the child sometimes experiences them. Deprivation and servitude are generally used *briefly* as the motivation for leaving home and getting the real tale under way.

Avoid becoming a bedtime roving reporter of today's fad tragedy, some bent calamity that gets so much attention not because it is prevalent but because it satisfies some people's baser curiosities and sells papers.

That said, give the hero's condition some time as you start the story. Usually this involves describing where the hero lives. Take nature for your mental picture. Do you want to have the animal live where it naturally does, or could your hero live in a house, like a mouse or a dog? Perhaps you'd enjoy creating an imaginary environment for your story. I have created tales set in a pillow factory run by a cat who has a clever mouse, Feathersack, for a neighbor; the mouse lives way down deep in a big bag of stuffing, her room lined with colorful feathers she has treasure-hunted from the supply right under the cat's nose. As you invent your hero's home, be free, be outlandish, stretch things a little — it is more fun and leads you places.

As for the character's parents, I think that the absence of parental figures is sometimes a very good way to create sympathy for the hero and avoid the confusing and delicate crosscurrents between you the storyteller and you the parent. The beginner should also avoid trying to create the complex split personalities and stepparents of fairy tales. They are enormously wise tales, and I encourage you to read them as inspiration, but you need to start with your area of competence and not try to invent "Cinderella" the first night. That story probably took two hundred years to evolve by the time Disney got hold of it and changed it substantially. Read it, think about it, but don't try to create it the first time you start this project.

You have to decide for yourself whether you want

to create an orphaned creature — literature is full of them — or whether you'd rather just put the parents at a distance. That is up to you. But the point is that this is the hero's story, not the parents'. You don't need to worry about feeding your child a fear of separation, by the way, because most likely your child is already haunted by it. It comes with birth and stays with us all our lives in one way or another. And a good deal of storytelling — with its great healing and encouraging messages for children — has to do with its power to suggest how children can handle this concern, what they can do about it, what stages they have to go through to become self-sustaining individuals, capable of adult decisions and relationships. If there is a parental figure in the story, constantly solving the problems for the hero, this tends to tell the child that he or she can't make it without the parent, that the child is utterly dependent. Ultimately, that is very discouraging news for everyone concerned.

As for siblings in your story, it is generally best to make them older because this makes your hero the youngest one. In a story, your child understands "the youngest one" as symbolic for the one who is miserable, the one who feels underappreciated, denied, second-fiddled, or any of a multitude of emotionally one-down situations which all children feel, regardless of birth order. The youngest one is the most sympathetic character, the one whose condition your child is going to identify with, even if he or she is the first-born. Also, on a practical note, if you have only one child, you will, obviously, be less likely to tell sibling stories. Sibling stories usually spring from a larger family context.

But if you do want to tell a sibling story, here are some suggestions. Siblings can be the sharers of an adventure or trial, or they can be the reason the hero sets out on a journey alone, to follow after the older ones or to retrieve them from some dire strait. Since I have twins, I have never used twins in my stories — I think it gets too close for my comfort and freedom — but twins represent a very close bond and suggest great mutual love. If you use twin heroes in your story, it seems to me, your story not only could involve those two characters as they are but also may involve two representative aspects of your single listener, picturing the male and female aspects of us all, the light and the dark, the shy and the outgoing, the unity of opposites, whatever plays in your child.

Parents want to foster good relations between their children, and so I think you will instinctively make your sibling stories ones in which both win together. It makes no sense for you to defeat one sibling, the one your child may actually wish was in Timbuktu right this minute, in favor of another. Sometimes the simplest way to deal with siblings in a story is to create characters who are not siblings at all. For instance, create a variety of animals, give them a common adversary, goal, history, or dilemma, give them a reason to work together, showing their individuality and differences as they do so, all at a distance from parents.

One day when Scoot was riding the white-capped waves away from his mother, he met a school of lantern fish swimming in a zigzag just under the surface.

The teacher called him. "We're having a counting lesson. We tried to count the waves but they won't hold still. There aren't any rocks on the bottom and we couldn't possibly count the sands. Can you think of anything else to count?"

"How 'bout my spots," said Scoot with a flourish of his tail.

As the school gathered around him, he held very still, and they counted 333 spots.

"One good deed deserves another," they called as he swam away. "We will remember you."

Give your hero a remove from his family, a sympathetic condition, care about him, bring him alive with an action or two, and you're on your way to the next part of the story.

(2) who had reason to set out on a journey

It is motivation time in the story. What in the hero's condition or qualities or state of mind might get him going out into the world? What reason can you create for the departure? The primal one — the one even babies understand — is hunger, but hunger has many mouths. It could be simple oral hunger, or it could be hunger for adventure, for a home of his own, for a playmate, for beauty, tolerance, knowledge, freedom — hunger for an infinite number of things. Think about your children and what they are drawn to. What do they desire at this stage in life? Get your feet wet on territory that you have walked during the day with them. To find the motivation for your hero's journey and to find the mood that surrounds him, think of your own child. What are the particular appetites you have noticed in him or her? Go ahead and make the instinctive call, play your hunch, and trust your own observations. No one knows your child better than you do. It is always appropriate to think about the motivation for the hero's action by asking yourself, "What is the yearning here in my child? What does the hero need to get going?"

I find fairy tales to be boundless inspirations because they are so intricate and so rich in motivation. Hansel and Gretel are moved by a desperate hunger in and around them; hunger and growth pervade this masterpiece of a tale. The boy in "The White Snake," prompted by curiosity, eats a bite of the king's secret dinner and sets out to grow up. The hero in "The Three Feathers" is motivated by a desire to earn his father's respect. The goose girl's maturation begins when she is careless with a handkerchief her mother gives her as she leaves home. The motivation for your hero to set out on a journey can be hunger, curiosity, need for respect and maturity, responsibility, or carelessness. And these are but a few of the classic motivations.

The reason for my hero to set out on a journey is often curiosity, a quality universal to children. Since you do not know where you are going with your initial stories — or, in the last analysis, with any of them — use curiosity as your touchstone and let it motivate your character to action in the first few stories. It puts your hero in a mood to travel, doesn't set you or the child into thorny, questionable paths to start out, and is an acceptable motive for both children and parents.

Later, of course, you will want to explore other motives for setting out on the mythical journey, leaving the path or the nest. I often have found that the motives I ascribe to my hero are in fact some of the emotions and values I honor. The natural surfacing of my values or concerns usually begins to take place about here in the story, when the hero is in the mood to travel. Perhaps the mouse hears a cry for help and rushes out into something unknown. Perhaps the dog feels lonely and wants to be with something other than people all the time. Here's the place in your story where you begin the real adventure, get your hero packing and moving down the road.

When he told his mother about the lantern fish, she said proudly that someday he would join a school, too. His heart sank. He didn't want to join a school. The fish in schools never seemed to be with their parents. To leave his mother for hours and stay in some group and go wherever it went — whether he wanted to or not — confused and alarmed him.

What motivates the hero in good storytelling is not always benign and desirable from the parents' standpoint. Little Red Riding Hood is disobedient when she strays off the path in search of pretty flowers, as is the son in "The Spirit in the Bottle" when he goes into the forest against his father's wishes; at the beginning of "The Frog-King," a girl makes a promise she has no intention of keeping. These naughty behaviors motivate the tales and at the same time create in the listening child a sympathetic response. I have yet to meet a child whose eyes don't sparkle on hearing about a little no-no someone *else* pulled off. It is up to you to decide what is sanctioned misbehavior and what is dangerous permission, but we parents should be realistic about our children and make some stories that acknowledge

misbehavior, ignorance, or carelessness as a motivation. We tell the child, indirectly, that we are not completely off the page as to the child's proclivities.

My characters, my heroes, however, usually set out
with good intentions, even though good intentions
may get them into trouble from which they must later
extricate themselves. I think this is true about the motivations of children. They almost never set out to get
into trouble and difficulty; in fact, they are most often
very surprised when troubles loom. So, I have never
sent a hero out maliciously looking for trouble or re-
venge. Nor have I sent one out looking for some fancy
abstraction like justice, peace, or truth. These are just
not part of my schedule of immediate motivations, any
more than they are for children. Great ideas like peace
and justice, however, may come at the *end* of the story,
or with the accumulation of stories over time. In the
same vein, I don't send heroes out into the world to
earn money, because money is, among other things, a
symbol of security for adults. If the story is actually
evolving as I tell it into a study of security, then I
patiently wait for my imagination to bring me an object other than money that symbolizes security for my
child. If it doesn't arrive as I speak the next words, I
wait and meander a bit on the character and his condition until it occurs to me — for instance, that my
child's security right at the moment is in the warmth
of his bed. With that snippet, I can begin to create
something about the unacceptability, the temporary
insecurity, of the hero's bed. Perhaps it has gotten
soggy from a rain storm, or ice has grown over it while
he was out, or some other animal has come and eaten
part of it, or whatever comes to mind. And then the

motivation of securing a warm, welcoming bed becomes enough for me to proceed with the story that discusses security.

Putting our hero in the mood to travel often stems from that greatest motivator of all, emotion or emotional conflict.

Scoot went off alone to worry. He didn't want to join a school — he wanted to be free, free to ride the boat waves, free to wave at the people, free to make wonderful leaps in the air. The bright sun did nothing for his spirits; the whispering seaweed annoyed him. He swam down to the deep, dark water where he could be alone with his troubles.

And now, because I have created in the story a likable hero who has a motivation to move or to travel, the story begins to have its own life.

(3) when a threat occurred

Every story must have a threat, a challenge, a difficulty. Life is full of them. I frankly don't think a story can claim the name if it doesn't contain a difficulty of some kind. Without a threat, it is a lullaby or a mood piece, not a story. And in case you are wary of imagining threats for your children and making their lives more burdensome, you must realize that to pretend that difficulties do not exist in the world is to utterly lie to your children, and children are the first to know it.

So, go ahead, tell the truth. Adversity is the name of the game at this stage in the story. Now, you have to judge how gentle or subtle, scary or awful you want this threat to be to your hero. You don't need to be mollycoddling and overprotective with your child, because his or her own imaginings are pretty dreadful too. I think you can safely go ahead, get into it. Cartoons have threats in them, movies do, and your children are exposed to them often. The point is not that you make up a threat or a monster — children are quite capable of doing that on their own — but rather that you bring adult insight into the threat and resolve it. To resolve it, to give it meaning, manageability, even defeat, is something you can do better than your child can. Your adulthood gives you insight that your child wants, insight that will give your child confidence in the face of his or her puzzlement with the world.

What I will say about the limits of threat, however, is that the threat you create must be a difficulty from which there is an escape for the hero. I am not advocating nuclear war here. I don't want you to drive yourself or your child into a brick wall. I'm talking about difficulty, even horrible difficulty, but there must be a way out. And, in fact, in imagination there always *is* a way out.

Deeper and deeper he went, down to the dark bottom where the sponges grew and the sun barely reached. As he moped at the mouth of a cave, not even wondering what could be in there, a sudden burst of grayness shot out, and a huge octopus with snakelike legs seized him, spurting a cloud of black ink. Scoot was terrified. He couldn't see, but he could feel the legs with horrible sucker cups sticking to him. He struggled with all his might against the coiling, tightening legs.

If your imagination is working honestly and easily, something will come to you in the process of describing the threat that will serve as your answer to the problem. Or something will have been laid down in the character of the hero — for instance, how smart he was, or how fast, or how he could slip through the narrowest cracks — that will serve as the hero's secret weapon against disaster. If you don't have the solution as you are describing the threat — which you probably won't — just wait. Wander and explore the threat for a while. Remember to *stay in the story*. Make little imaginative forays into corners of the burrow, or the feelings of the mouse or dog or brown-eyed hero, wander around to whatever strikes you, and after a few seconds, which may in fact seem like hours, your imagination will hand you the solution.

(4) from which there was a hero-inspired way out

All you need is a glimpse of the answer in your imagination as you talk out loud, and the story will really start to fly here in the fourth part. This is the climax of the storyteller's energy, for as you come to the answer that fits the story and fits your child, even though you will not be analyzing the story from this basis, you will intuitively know when you have hit on the needed escape. It is often the first solution that pops into your mind when you realize you've got to get your hero out of this fix.

I feel quite strongly that the escape mechanism is best found in the nature of the hero, not in some outside force that comes in and waves a wand or acts like a parent in some way, protecting, saving the hero/

child. Remember, this is a success story for your child. The hero has to have some quality or some clever idea that extricates him from the trouble, something that comes with his body, mind, spirit, or ongoing actions, from his actual nature, that leads to the defeat of the threat. Again, the hero can be small, with the advantages of smallness. The hero can be clever or intelligent about the habits of his adversary, and win with mind. If the temperament of the hero is one of slow and steady effort, like the tortoise, persistence too can win the race. If the hero has been constantly making an effort of some kind, has been studying or practicing something, or has observed the failures and foibles of others, those too can be turned to the uses of victory.

Allow me a brief digression on wand-waving fairy godmothers here. Although Disney made a wonderful movie of "Cinderella," he took away some of the power Cinderella had in the original story. In the Grimm brothers' version, Cinderella never has a fairy godmother, a smug, pudgy female all twinkle and squeak, giggling as she transforms Cinderella and the pumpkin, as though they were of the same caliber. Also, Disney neglected to mention that Cinderella had been visiting her dead mother's grave three times a day since her death. I suspect the motivation for this omission at the studios was to protect our children's tender sensibilities, but more truthfully — to the bone of it — to avoid our own adult, parental fear of death. In Grimm's, Cinderella has been going to her mother's grave and weeping on a hazel branch she'd asked her father to bring her from his travels (the stepsisters asked for, and *got*, dresses and jewels). Watered with her tears, the branch takes root on the grave, and a little white bird lands on the tree each day and grants her whatever she wishes. When the stepmother promises Cinderella she may go to the ball if she accomplishes impossible tasks (in which hundreds of birds assist Cinderella's success), the cruel woman says, "All this will not help; you cannot go with us, for you have no clothes and cannot dance; we should be ashamed of you!"

So Cinderella goes to her mourning place and says to the bird, "Shiver and quiver, my little tree, / Silver and gold throw down over me." And the bird delivers not only the dress but slippers embroidered with silk and silver. And Cinderella goes to the festival on her own two feet — no pumpkin chariot, no glass slippers. She takes charge in this story. I think it is a much more satisfying version, much more "liberated," than Disney's. And it comes from centuries past!

This digression underscores my point: let the hero escape on his or her own. Let the hero have the magic wand, the silver axe, the invisible cloak; don't give them to parental fairy figures. Let the hero's emotions bring forth the wonders and enchantment in the story; let the hero mourn, if that is necessary, for something will come of it. Let the hero have emotions that your child has. Let the hero *act*. A white bird, capable of granting wishes, can appear through the grace of the hero's daily efforts, requests, and actions, but cannot come, *deus ex machina*, down into the middle of the story. Escape and consolation come, in my book, from within the hero. Because — applying the golden rule here — I, just like children, want to hope that I will not forever be dependent on the shaky benevolence of others in power. It's not too much to hope for, independence. It should be in your story. It is part of the quest.

Now, escape or recovery from a threat may be represented in your story by other characters, like the white bird. The difference between the white bird and the fairy godmother in Disney is that the godmother comes from nowhere, while the white bird is attached to the persona of Cinderella; the bird has sprung from her visits to the grave and her request for the hazel branch, which she has tended for a long time. White birdlike creatures don't simply arrive like the grace of God, but rather come because of the slowly rooting hazel tree and the ongoing actions of the girl; from her constant weeping and daily efforts and hard work comes a glorious symbol of self-expansion. The bird was a part of Cinderella in a magical way, had sprung from her character.

You don't have to invent white birds all the time in order to save your hero. You may want to create extensions of the hero with other animals that are linked to him in the story by his actions. These helpful animals represent the hero's inner resources. A good example of this is in the Grimm's story "The White Snake." A boy steals a bite of the king's secret dinner — a white snake — and is driven from the castle on horseback to find his way in the world. As he steers his horse away from a little nation of ants, they cry out to him that he will be remembered for sparing them. "One good turn deserves another," they shout, and indeed, later in the story, when the princess tests him by strewing ten sacksful of millet seed on the grass to be picked up before sunrise and "not a single grain be wanting," how does he manage this impossible task? His buddies the ants come in the night, thousands of little hero-extensions, who by "great industry picked up all the millet-seed and gathered them into the sacks."

Take this as a pattern. If you want your hero to be extricated by others, there are many creatures which, in stereotype, express human qualities that can be extensions of the hero. Ants symbolize earthy industriousness, fishes can dive deep into the mysterious sea for the golden ring, ravens can fly through the air to the end of the earth for the apple of life, and so on. (In Chapter 9 I'll talk more about such symbols.) Give these animals a special connection with the hero — gratitude being the classic one — and they will help do the work the hero needs done, and the hero, in the child's mind, still gets the credit.

Deep in the cave, the school of lantern fish heard his cries and came swirling out all around him. They knew this octopus too well. They knew what to do. Thousands of little fins and tails fanned with such energy that they blew the ink away. Now Scoot could see the monster's fleshy head and how his legs were wrapped. He thought, "Somersault! Slide!" And with a sudden jerk and a marvelous twirl of his spotted back, he rolled and slid from the grasp of the octopus, like a bubble from a wand.

These hero-extensions are on the advanced side, but you will create them sooner than you think. When you are starting out, simply deal with the animal hero as is. Let muscle, fleetness, cleverness, slipperiness, acuity of senses, smallness, color, or temperament of the hero be the source of the victory. This is immensely satisfying to the child. But by now, you understand why.

Another way to deal with the threat is to turn it

upon itself. Justice is a very important thing to children. I believe it is one of their first moral understandings, and comes because children are so aware of their small share of fair treatment in the world. They are deeply satisfied when your tale ends justly, because they often feel unfairly treated in real life. How regularly they dispute our directions; how consistently they quibble amongst themselves over who gets the big piece; how instinctively they watch us for glimmers of favoritism.

In the traditional fairy tale, the hero is rewarded and the villain meets his well-deserved fate, often defeated by his own evil method, like the witch in "Hansel and Gretel." At the end, children feel relief that justice has prevailed and are not, at their young age, particularly concerned about mercy. That inclination requires some guilty, flawed, gray-toned, worldly-wise living.

In *The Uses of Enchantment*, Bruno Bettelheim says: "Adults often think that the cruel punishment of an evil person in fairy tales upsets and scares children unnecessarily. Quite the opposite is true; such retribution reassures the child that the punishment fits the crime. The child often feels unjustly treated by adults and the world in general, and it seems that nothing is done about it. On the basis of such experiences alone, he wants those who cheat and degrade him . . . severely punished. If they are not, the child thinks that nobody is serious about protecting him."

To put it simply, evil is a big problem in this old world. In spite of one witch's demise, it seems that evil cannot be burnt out of this animal species of ours, a fact that even the most gloating, revenge-satisfied child would probably grant. Nevertheless, I am big on giving

evil characters in my stories the heave-ho. I choose —
and I realize it is a choice — to go on the premise that
goodness will prevail and justice will be done to evil-
doers, especially if the good ones pay attention and are
willing to act. Gretel was paying attention and acted
and won. I think I've learned something from Gretel.

So when you create the threat in your story,
whether it is a predatory creature, a machine, a villain,
or an octopus, think about how you are willing to bring
justice to this villain. A good way is to imagine the
Achilles' heel of the bad guy. There is always a weak-
ness to any strength. If the adversary is ice, ice can be
melted; if it is fire, fire can be smothered. It's like the
"scissors, paper, rock" game: paper covers rock, rock
smashes scissors, scissors cut paper. Let your imagination and your memory work together as you create this
part of the story. Ask yourself, what of this threat is
mutable, changeable? Where is the switch that can be
thrown, the clever trick that can turn the threat upon
itself? The devouring witch dies in her own oven; the
cruel, vain queen in "Snow White" dies dancing in red-
hot iron slippers that have been put in the fire; her
jealousy of youth is her undoing. Try to make the
punishment fit the crime. It doesn't always have to be
awful.

Your little animal hero can defeat the threat without
blood on his hands. Do what you believe is right, just,
fair. Let your own values guide you. Perhaps the quality that enables the hero to escape is strength, perhaps
it is fluidity, perhaps it is persistence, or honesty, or
discipline. Or just let the hero's native intelligence take
action in your story.

Then, with amazing speed, Scoot swam round and

round the thrashing body of the beast, making such powerful circles that the water whirled, shoved, whacked, against the monster's legs until they were tangled into useless, sticky, hard knots.

Agility, whether physical or mental, is a wonderful winning quality. I happen to value intelligence, common sense, thought in life, so, as often as not, I give my hero an agile mind. Remember the story about the car wash? Resourceful Feathersack used her head, controlled the machine, and won a victorious return to her home.

(5) which resulted in a safe return and a happy ending

In the end, the hero, having escaped the octopus, defeated the witch, or switched off the car wash, returns to a safe, familiar place. Home. This is a very necessary ending to any adventure story for children, because a home is utterly necessary to their survival. I always have my hero come home at the end. I do not believe in never-ending stories that leave the hero lost in the stars, walking an endless road with shirttails flapping. Rather, I bring my heroes to their nests, to their cozy beds, to the welcome of their family, or whatever seems nice that night. The story is still in a land of imagination, but this is the place in the story where the surface of real life begins to show over the heads of us all in that storytelling room. As though looking up from underwater, seeing my air bubbles rise to the top, I know, as the storyteller, I am about to come up for air.

Sometimes, if the child is old enough, I may spend a moment spinning out the victory, letting something besides the warm, safe bed be the reward. Because, like justice, reward is very important to good stories. Sometimes in fairy tales a shower of gold or pearls and jewels come down on the hero. And this is fine, but it has to come from within the story. Again, the reward does not come down like a diamond bracelet on a wire, from some unconnected personage in the story. Hansel and Gretel find the witch's hoard in her house and fill their pockets with riches, and this reward in the context of the great starving poverty of the story is apt and pleasing; they return to their father and "all anxiety is at an end." But I'm not a believer in material rewards for courage, nor are fairy tales always devoted to this ending. In "Rapunzel," the prince's blindness is cured by Rapunzel's tears; in "Brother and Sister," the siblings live happily together all their lives. There are many satisfying endings. And as you practice, you will use some of them instinctively.

I must tell you that I have gone heavy on the reward side of parenting and storytelling. I believe that a child so wants to please us that when he or she does, we should be quick to acknowledge and praise it. It's a much more pleasant way of molding behavior than taking out the guidebook to punishment; I look for opportunities to reward my children. That is why I always end my stories with a reward for the hero and perhaps, spend more time on it than other storytellers might. I think this part of the story is an opportunity to tell my children what things I feel to *be* rewarding: unhurried time together, a big hug, warmth, beauty, celebration, a bowl of soup . . . The list could go on for pages.

I have generally rewarded my heroes with something I know my child imaginatively understands as a comforting, pleasant, valuable reward. It could be a nibble of clover or a huge patch of wild strawberries for a hungry rabbit; it could be a joyful flag over the long-lost house, or an exhilarated, triumphant exhaustion that leads to deep and restful sleep under covers made all of velvet. It could be the perfect full moon shining over the pond, or a family celebration for the hero's safe return, complete with music, games, and chocolate chip cookies. These last rewards verge on the realistic rather than the symbolic, because this is the part of the story that must begin to return to the real world, the room where we recline, the night air that we actually breathe. Most of all I make the hero return to loving relationships, safe quarters, peace of mind. I do this because I want my children to sleep well. And, as I leave them, I hope they will savor the security and confidence that come from vicarious accomplishment and courage. In the solitary lull before sleep, I hope they will reflect on the story with peaceful thoughts.

And when Scoot got home, his blood was pounding with joy and relief. Every coral, every shell in his home looked more beautiful than before. He nudged his mother's nose and told her all about the octopus and the lantern fish and his somersault. She listened intently, relieved and proud.

"I think a school could be fun," he told her. "You make friends there."

His mother smiled gently and patted his head with her flipper. "With a smile like yours, you'll make many friends, I'm sure."

And so, in their home in the deeps, while they

waited for the moon to rise over the sea, they drifted together, side by side. As night came on and he began to feel drowsy, the little dolphin listened to the seaweed's hush and to the waves above him singing, "Wish, wish, wish."

What is important to remember is that the finest moment in a bedtime story is when life is revealed as a glorious gift, a wondrous adventure, an eccentric pleasure in which, after difficulties are faced and overcome, the heroes gain a higher ground and are more self-confident in their ability to pursue happiness as they define it.

With the safe return home, with a reward, I then end the enchantment. I feel this moment when it comes. There is nothing more to be said, the hero is home, not necessarily safe forevermore because tomorrow I will bring a new threat or challenge or adversity to my hero. But for now, all is well. I take a deep breath and let the last words stay in the air a moment, and then I simply say, "The end."

After the story, I kiss my child, adjust the covers, and leave. I do not explain the story. If the story is well formed, the child is content to have me leave. If there is a flaw in the story and the child notes it, I make a brief explanation and chalk it up to experience. I know my imagination will work on more variations tomorrow, and I will come up with another story, perhaps better than this one was.

So, steadfastly, night after night, you and your heroes will work in your own small, gentle, tentative ways against a sea of troubles. Night after night some strength, wisdom, insight, some small encouraging victory, some delightful escape and safe return will occur in your story, if you trust your imagination. Night after night your child senses a bit of the "rapture of being alive" as the hero comes home. And night after night you will approach something dormant and unconscious in your nature, and find, in little ways, that you are enacting some of the truths that are fundamental to our being human — deeper than you might give yourself credit for. You will go through those "fragrant portals, dimly starred," into and out of the land of enchantment. And night after night your child will say to you, "Tell me a story out of your mind."

◆ The only gift is a portion of thyself.
    — *Ralph Waldo Emerson*

7

Values, Persistence, and Trumpets: Your Child's Hope in an Uncertain World

◆ ◆ YOU DON'T HAVE to set them in stone, make a list, or get pedantic about it, but as you set out to tell stories, many of your principles and attitudes about life are going to instinctively come into play as you start to explore storytelling. This is very welcome news. Don't be surprised when they arrive, be grateful. I cannot say specifically what they will be because, obviously, they are what *you* believe in. Whether or not you've thought about them, your values are going to appear as motivations, solutions, and rewards within the tales you tell. And your child, deep down, anxiously awaits them.

Although I seldom set out to tell a story about a value, I find that often, behind the action and characters of my stories, my values keep surfacing like white-finned goldfish in a Chinese bowl, coming up to the surface for air and then swimming down again, all shimmering, elusive, and lovely to watch in the water. Strangely, wonderfully, my inner voice comes up with symbols for virtues or principles I have already chosen to embrace that afternoon or for my lifetime. I believe it will work this way with you too.

If you are big on independence and freedom, those values will come up in your stories. You may find yourself telling tales about pioneers, deep-sea divers, orphans, trailblazers, astronauts, inventors, artists.

If you trust in hard work and study, those will arrive. You may invent laboratories for your characters, magic books, or intense peerings into enchanted telescopes. You may find yourself creating stories that pass over years, with the hero slowly working to the top of the mountain or to the inner mystery of the iceberg, an emerald, or a galaxy.

If you believe in aggressively going after the goal, getting in the game, that will surface. Perhaps you have in you a few yarns of the football field, the magic helmet, the mitt that could catch anything, even dreams. You'll find yourself making stories about heroes who compete against great odds, bump against adversity, and win glorious boons.

If you want justice or kindness in the world, they will arrive in your stories. You may invent characters with huge hearts or fair minds, the bottomless soup bowl, the drawer who had enough clothes for the whole world, the cloud who rained on dishonesty, or the kindest safety pin on earth who could make any hole whole.

If you value the golden rule, forgiveness, listening, beauty, democracy, charity, the free market, encouragement, law, medicine, or music, your heroes will use what you value. The list is inexhaustible.

Your values will apply to any part of the story: the hero's attributes, the motive for action, the resolution of the trouble. You can revel, roll around in the easy truth that what you count as necessary, important, quintessential, sweet, powerful, winning, or eternal will happen in your stories, almost without your thinking about it.

As your values naturally become woven into your tales, I think something else will happen too: they will take on different shapes, depending on the situation, the depth of the water in your story, so to speak. Your imagination will interpret your values, give them objective form, which will cause you to later wonder about what you have invented. For instance, I can now wonder why I take the abstract notion of values and characterize them as beautiful golden fish, which leads me to think, well, goldfish, like values, are domestic, vulnerable, beautiful, and so on. Is that a good symbol for values? Do I in fact think that values are so fragile? Perhaps I should have them be gilded whales in the sea. And what about the water in the Chinese bowl where they swim? Is the water my unconscious, as some people say? Do I think that important virtues reside in the unconscious, inner waters of our minds, waiting to be hooked? Why is my bowl Chinese and so small compared with the sea? My images raise questions for me to ponder.

All I know is that the value that appears on your forehead for the duration of a story changes shape and is seen more complexly through your imagination. You will find that you will begin thinking, questioning, correcting, refining your values as months go by, for yourself and for your child. This is a wonderful fact, a source of growth for both of you.

Let's say one night you tell a story about a dog who gets lost; perhaps it came spinning off a day at Christmastime in an immense toy store packed with strangers when you and your child became separated. On the night of that experience you decide to imaginatively tell your child about what to do if he or she becomes lost somewhere. You invent an appealing cinnamon-colored dog, soft-furred, curious, and happy, who leaves her father's side, following the scents of sleeping squirrels, stray tennis balls, and pine, and gets lost in the forest. She cannot find her way out and begins to run in every direction, whimpering, barking, to no avail, until she realizes that her father will look for her, she *knows* he will. She stops to think: if she keeps running around, her father will have a hard time finding her. So the little dog decides to just sit down and not move, to wait. And of course, her father, whose nose is every bit as good as hers is, finds her and takes her back home safely in the end.

It is a fine story, a fine message, and you say good night. But perhaps there is something missing for you in that story. It lingers, the gap, the inadequacy. You reflect on how horrible and serious lostness is, not always solved by just sitting down and waiting for Dad or Mom. You find that you want to say more about it; more than just waiting and patience, you realize that lostness sometimes needs action, not passivity. And so another night you revise the story, adding a wise robin in the forest who knows the trees and flies overhead, leading the dog home (to stand for a hero-extension in the store who gets on the microphone and makes an announcement about a lost child). Or you offer the little dog's native ability to smell or bark her way back, and when she does, she decides to stay closer from now on (emphasizing the child's ability to save herself).

What I mean to illustrate is that your values and your principles will become sharper, more refined, as you tell stories, because stories gently question the storyteller and elicit clearer thinking and truer searching. If, for instance, you were raised to believe that all people are good and blithely offer that as a solution in one of your stories, you may find, as you think about it in the cold light of dawn, that you no longer believe all people *are* good. Then you have to correct that in your stories too. Don't give your children canned values. Try to keep them as fresh and honest as you can. Just as you correct your beliefs and make them more your own, so too will you make better and better stories for your children.

Make Your Hero Persistent

There is only one value which I believe belongs in everyone's stories, and that is persistence. By that I don't mean something dogged, blind, habitual, me-

chanical, but rather a quiet awareness that just getting
up in the morning, day after day, is a kind of persistence, getting up with a willingness to go on with it all,
with a hope that today may bring progress, small as it
usually is. Persistence is a value all children need.
Since the ultimate purpose of your stories is to assure
your children that they will indeed succeed in the task
of growing up in this uncertain world — that you are
convinced of it — it is important never to let a problem
totally overwhelm your hero. In every story you must
show your child that the character with whom he or
she identifies has to struggle too, but after one or two
or — classically — three efforts, the hero's persistence
will result in at least some forward motion or, at best,
victory.

Realistically, some problems — death, human limi-
tations, natural catastrophe — cannot be solved; nevertheless, you should tell your children that if they
persevere against unfair troubles, even catastrophes,
they will find meaning in life, learn something important, and succeed in the lifelong task of growing up.
Tell them you believe they will be able to handle even
the bad things that must inevitably come. And give
them a hand with the task by describing the values that
have helped you to confront, bear, and interpret suffering or difficulty as you have experienced it.

Perhaps your stories will offer *active*-value solutions; for instance, mixtures of education, physical
self-reliance, civilization, attack and defense; or *inner*-
value solutions: potions of thought, reflection, courage, and intuition; or *emotional*-value solutions: perhaps a bouquet of hope, love, and forgiveness; or
spiritual-value solutions: an honoring of the mysteri-

ous, the religious, or the peace of the passage of time. But, no matter what, please make your little hero persist against trouble, lean into it and make some headway. Children — looking up through what seem endless years before maturity — must be told that their efforts will finally show some achievement, increased power, and growth. I know that if I tell my children that with persistence they will find some meaning in it all, they will have a better shot at it. The more of us who spend some time with these concerns, the more likely the positive values the race holds dear will be passed on and advanced in our many children.

Your stories can transform your wisdom and experience into a shape that your children can imaginatively get their arms around. If you are able to raise a real baby, you are able to give it what meaning you have come to know, limited though it inevitably is. Your stories will inform your child about your most personally held convictions and perhaps about some of your weaknesses too. And that's all right. You have to believe that you are respectable enough to offer yourself to them as you are, because children eventually know, anyway, if you fake it. Your values, like mine, are not the last answer, but they are what make life meaningful, accessible, successful for you. Children cannot really know you if all you show them is how to fold their clothes or how to read a clock. They want to know what wisdom you have; they know it is far greater than theirs. As you give them the love gift of an imaginative story, as you guide them with your values and understandings, you are putting another layer of beauty and mystery on your own relationship with them. You are willing to show them your values

— or have them revealed by accident — in a way that is not demanding or preachy.

Value Your Child's Input — Trumpets, Please!

Another thing I urge you to value, even put on a pedestal, is the personal wisdom that your child has about his or her own day. Children know what hits them, what matters to them. They live in their own sensations and experience, not yours, not society's. One of the great unsung triumphs of children is that their lives are open, available, on the surface, and ready to be said. With enviable concentration, with simple truth, they know themselves.

Value this. Honor it anytime, and know that on the practical level of storytelling it is sometimes a godsend. If you, as a storyteller, don't have a subject you want to explore, can't think of some ticklish event or experience to bounce your story off, simply say, "What would you like a story about?" The child will know right away. He or she may have been taken by the button that wouldn't behave, or the bubbles that slid down the side of the tub and vanished, or the dog that ran into the street.

It has been my experience that the question "What shall I make the story about?" is sometimes worth the information alone, never mind the story it inspires. When you ask a child for a subject or a situation worthy of a story, you will find that his or her ability to sort through the endless loop is better than yours, by a long shot. It makes me laugh, frankly, with delight and relief and love to say this to you. It is amazing how addled and scattered our minds can be, and how clear, refreshing, and pure theirs are. If we ask children a voluminous question, like what the story should be about, they have a simple, usually instantaneous, entirely without intellectualizing, terrific idea. It just comes to them, and they never think to doubt it. It hasn't occurred to them to struggle, as we do, to come up with the most important, charming, or frustrating thing about their day. If you want to tell a story, ask your child to guide you. The best way for the child is the child's way, when it comes to the inspiration of the story. This should be a hearty comfort for you as a beginning storyteller, having an idea-maker right there, wearing slipper socks and smelling of toothpaste.

Defining a Family — Adoptive, Single, or Step Parents

As you settle into that lovely pause when your child is in bed and a story is about to begin, you may find that your toothpaste-fragrant guide will ask you to tell a story about your family. Family is the most fundamental need your child has, after all. For your child, food, clothing, and shelter presume the presence of your family.

Ever since the word was invented, each generation has tried to figure out what "family" means. Is it kinship, a shared roof, a common ancestor, the same values, a bond carried entirely in the heart? Each of us has a personal definition. But as the definition expands or contracts from one individual to another — like an accordion — it makes music either way. Family, no matter how it is defined in this uncertain world, is a necessity to your children.

Many parents today have remarried and mingled their children in the same household; others are single and are going solo with children; others have adopted children. Each of these relationships, and others as well, constitutes a family, and each can be symbolized and affirmed with imaginative stories. "How One Family Came to Be" is a worthy tale, one which is important to both children and parents.

But sometimes, approaching such a tale puts us in a quandary. How close to the facts should fantasy come? How much distance should this tale have from our real world? One parent might wonder, "How can I tell a positive story about stepparents, given all the lingering connotations of the term?" Another might say, "How can I assure my children that even though they are not my flesh and blood, I am their true parent?" Another might ask, "How can I say that one loving parent is plenty?"

I cannot create the right story for you — as you well know — because lives are too particular, children too distinct, and nobody knows your child better than you do. But if you create stories about your specific family, the key word to keep in mind is "love." Every good basic story — regardless of the biological relationship between the teller and the child — is about a hero who overcomes a difficulty and returns to the love and protection of home. By creating symbols and happy endings, you can speak tenderly to your child about real-life issues.

I would suggest, however — since this is such an important kind of story — that you tell a series of stories, not necessarily all in a row; don't become fixated on a single theme. Yet there are seasons in a child's life when this question is important, and other times when it is a deep and personal concern to you. Both are proper times to creatively express your love and hope for your child. You will give wiser, more subtle interpretations of your family if you approach it with a collection of stories.

Your tales — whether about the configurations of your family or about a thousand other issues in your lives — will honor and value the questions your child most deeply wants to know: "Am I loved? Can I make it? Will you take care of me?" And your very valuable answer is simply — yes.

The Value of Fantasy

While you are sorting through your values, looking for the ones that are closest to your center, know that if you asked your children to do the same thing, they would probably put fantasy or imagination right there in the middle of things they use every day in order to get by. They know that fantasy is part of their inner reality. So, as you go into the world of imagination, you are echoing your children's way of dealing with the world and telling them that their natural way is acceptable to you. You, in the temporary guise of a magician or a wizard, will be entering a world your children count on, listen to. Children spend a lot of time with their imaginations, and fantasy sometimes makes things acceptable if nothing else works. They know it is another way of looking for meaning.

Some parents are afraid of this fact and worry that their child is going off the deep end with fantasy. That is only rarely a problem. All healthy children know the difference between fantasy and reality. Don't be afraid you are going to be opening a can of endless worms by affirming fantasy. A healthy child doesn't confuse it with external reality any more than you do. Your son may be pretending that a soap dish is a marvelous sailing boat — loaded with elephants for company, flapping flags for music, and hammocks for sleeping — but when the bath is over, he knows it for what it is and puts the soap in it.

Also, your stories are *contained* fantasy. They are formal, declared excursions into the world of enchantment; they have an end. As J. R. R. Tolkien, the author of *The Lord of the Rings*, said: "I never imagined that the dragon was of the same order as the horse. The dragon had the trademark Of Faerie written plainly upon him. In whatever world he had his being, it was of Other-world . . . I desired dragons with a profound desire. Of course, I in my timid body did not wish to have them in the neighborhood, intruding in my relatively safe world."

The real problem of fantasy with children is not that they have it but that they don't know where to take it, how to resolve it. This is where your worth as a storyteller is greatest. You know, because of your values, beliefs, and experience, what to do with fantasy: it has to be steered toward a solution, an understanding, a satisfactory ending. Therefore, don't let the child tell the whole story or you will both end up in a muddle. Children can imagine wonderful and terrible things, but they cannot figure out what to *value* in the midst of it all. In the wonderland or the dilemma, they don't know where to plug in the persistence. That is your job. It is up to you to build the story and the ending so that it turns out satisfactorily. While the fantasy is unreal, the message it gives your children about themselves and about their future is real: life — in this uncertain world, with all its difficulties — is exciting and hopeful. After the child has given you the idea, take charge of the story and trust that your values will arrive to serve you hand and foot.

♦ Nothing great was ever achieved without enthusiasm.
— *Ralph Waldo Emerson*

♦ Dullness is the chief enemy of art.
— *Brenda Ueland*

8

Style, Detail, and Burrs

♦ ♦ STYLE IS a very individual thing. What is most important about your stories is that they come from your voice, your imagination, your style. When you are in a clear, restful mood, spinning a story, making it up as you go, you don't want to interrupt yourself with a lot of clutter and self-criticism as to your style. You must just trust that you have one, and go with it. It will be fine. "Style" describes the kind of voice, slant, or tone that artists take in their work. I suppose I have a style, although I don't think about it as I write; it just comes from my manner of speaking and my manner of thinking. You read here the way my mind works. You will tell stories the way your mind works. It will be your style, your tone, and it is very valuable. Your style is the perfect one for your child.

The only time to think about style is when you realize that your stories must have one very important stylish thing: interest. As you start out telling stories, it isn't going to ruin your style to think about the clarity and content of your tales. Keep to your voice, think about what your child needs, use your imagination, remember your values too, but also try to set out with a commitment to telling a story that is *interesting* to your child. Boredom makes anyone fidget.

If the story is interesting and engaging, a great number of "errors" can occur in your tales and your child probably won't notice, or at least won't fidget; you can think about your story's flaws later and make improvements the next night. To make your stories interesting, I'd like to suggest some cautions and some attention-holders, some magic cards for you to hold while you tell your story.

The Magic of Detail

Detail is essential to interest. As I have already said, your description of your hero is all-important, and you should be determined to give him life by giving him specificity. To say your hero has blond hair is one thing, to say the hair was the color of gold is better, to say that the hair was so beautiful that butterflies were attracted to it is even better, for then you are verging on the magical with the detail. Let your mind go, and associate. Blond is yellow, the color of the sun, the color of corn, the color of lemonade, or the solemn color of the low moon. Blond hair is usually fine in texture, fine as silk thread, soft as goofer feathers, whatever. Or make your hero's hair brown and glowing, the color of caramel or chocolate, like joy in the hand, or full of curls that tumbled down like little songs upon his shoulders.

Use a detail that comes from your inner voice. Each of these details will probably suggest a theme for the hero's adventure, so pay attention, keep your antennae up. If your hero is a horse, don't make him just brown with a black mane. Elaborate. Perhaps your horse's neck arches so high and handsomely that there is no fence he could not see over, or the horse's tail is so strong that three boys could ride like the wind on it, or he wears silver shoes that make him the fastest horse in the land. Your detail not only makes your hero sympathetic, it also makes him special, specific, interesting. And the details give you material to work with later.

When you have gotten your hero into the land of enchantment, use a few real-life details in describing the environment. The magic is not lessened, by any means, and in fact becomes more eloquent, more riveting, if you have some microscopic, closely seen and described, truthful specific in your environment. For instance, if you are sending your hero into the woods, and the woods in your story represents confusion, spend a minute telling about the tangle. Elaborate on your symbol of the woods. You could say the bottom branches of the trees had no leaves and scratched like porcupine quills or kitchen forks; or that the burrs stuck to the hero's shoelaces and clothes like horrible insects; or that the trees were so close together it was like walking into someone else's jammed closet, and smelled funny. If you have your hero just entering the woods, take a minute to give a detail that comes from your real-life experience. Perhaps it will be that the hero, coming from the sunlight into the darkness, finds that her eyes are nearly blinded. She rubs them. And then, slowly, as her eyes adjust, the woods are not really dark and black but only a shadowy place where the grays of the ground become a dull green, dotted with acorns, and she can see the baby trees just sprouting through the pine needles, and she can even see a lovely feather of a blue jay lying on her path. Use detail to flesh out your story. Use it whenever it comes to you, and I can assure you it *will* come — that is what is so amazing about storytelling. Your details will actually lead you, the storyteller, on. For as that blue jay feather appears in your mind, with it an actual blue jay may appear who must become a part of your story. Every detail leads you on as well as making each instant of your story more alive and vivid.

When your hero is facing the threat, give it detail. Describe, for example, how the witch had one red eye, or the bear had claws that looked like the tines of a garden hoe, or the giant was so stupid that when the hero told him that his book bag was full of magic the giant's appetite for hero-flesh was changed to a desire for the magic contents. You see, the detail can inspire the story. If you come up with the idea of a magic backpack, you can do something with it. It leads on. What really *is* in the backpack? A sandwich, a spelling book, three pencils, and a lot of marked-up papers in a wad? Make it up. Imagine what is really in your child's backpack and then use it imaginatively. Go with it. The hero takes out a pencil and tells the stupid giant that this stick has written every book in the world and is mightier than the sword. Or this tuna fish sandwich came from the sea and contains the power of waves and storm. Or this wad of math papers is really the secret of going into business and making great wealth. Make it up. Have fun with it, let yourself go, be daring, be silly, exaggerate!

Use details when the threat is resolved. When the witch dies, perhaps her red eye flashes fire for a moment, then turns into a piece of charcoal; a little puff of smoke curls up from it and traces off in the air, blown to nothingness by the evening breeze. That's pretty descriptive. Or how about the bear's scary, curled claws, the ones like a garden hoe — why not have them get caught in the hero's power mower in the end and snipped off just like fingernails? You see, one detail leads to the next. If you are talking about garden tools when you first describe your threat, the bear's claws, you will come up with a resolution later that springs from the same toolshed: the power mower. Perhaps you would prefer something other than a power mower as you worry about your child revving up an engine the next day. Okay, make it a sickle or magic garden gloves or a can of bug spray that defeats the bear. You can think of plenty of things. Make them spring from earlier details. Make them fit your child, your values. The detail of claws being like tines leads to the solution. The detail of one red eye leads to thoughts of fire and how fire dies and gives you the next detail and the next, until the final one fixes the image of the witch's or bear's defeat with wonderful excitement.

When you bring the hero home, continue the detail

that has been tracing through your story. The backpack could feel like a feather on his now stronger shoulders; it once was as heavy as lead. The power mower could cut a path back home that is wide and smooth and easy to walk on, lined with ripe blackberries drooping on the canes. Or make up a new detail, for now that your hero is leaving the difficulty with a sense of victory and growth, you can change the stream of thought. You can bring in a detail that has to do with growth. Perhaps the hero's shoes feel too tight, or his little sweater hardly covers his elbows, or his legs make longer strides. Hansel and Gretel returned home by crossing a lake on the back of a white duck, one at a time, because "both of them would be too heavy for the little duck," says Gretel. Actually, crossing a body of water is symbolic of growth. On the other side of the water, in any story, the hero is more mature, more self-confident, knows better who he or she is. We cross water to a more mature awareness. I think children understand this intuitively. It is part of ancestral human memory, the picture-language.

Use whatever detail comes to you that night. Make it up. Perhaps there is something in the child's day that will occur to you as a detail about growth that gives interest to your story. For very young children, finding food along the way is a sign of greater self-sufficiency, as is knowing the way back home without anyone telling them. Sometimes just being able to reach the doorknob is enough.

When you create details, don't stint on the story or limit yourself by making them babyish. Lean toward the next phase in your child's understanding. Go into your imagination and give a detail that feels right to you, that comes from your adult mind. Your details can be more mature than your child is because story-telling is a very good way to stretch your child's vocabulary and awareness of things. Don't limit your language and talk down to your listener. Your child has learned to understand language itself, the meanings of words, by the context. We ask children to reach, to extend themselves linguistically, every day, in ordinary moments, so there is no reason to stop now. If the word "tine" is beyond them, don't censure it, give it a quick description and keep right on. It is the *idea* of tine, the descriptiveness of the word, that you want, and your child will happily follow you, learning something as the story grows, delighting in every detail.

Be Natural

Be yourself, be natural. Don't attempt to imitate or copy someone else's style. All of us have probably been transfixed by a person who can tell a good joke, but if you actually set out to imitate exactly how someone else did it, your rendition somehow is not as funny. You are stilted and self-conscious. The great joke teller was being very natural in his or her way of telling, and you cannot be natural yourself if you are busy thinking, "Now did he put his hand on top of his head here?" or "Is this the moment when she made that face that cracked me up? Shall I try to make the exact face?" While you are busy imitating, you are losing your own gestures, losing the rhythm, losing your own natural way of telling. Rather, take pains to admire what things were good in a general way, and then just do it as best you can, your way. Be engrossed in the joke on your own terms, with your own gestures and pacing. And people will laugh.

Just as you should not try to utterly imitate another's joke, I also think it is inappropriate for you to use dialect in your stories unless it is your own. "Now, b'rer fox, he lay low" is a wonderful line, and we all probably delight in having heard Uncle Remus say it. It was natural to him, or we are led to believe it was. Speaking in dialect is delightful if it is your dialect or that of your family. It can preserve something very valuable in the human race to use your ancestor's way of speech and pass it on to your children. But using the dialect of others whose cultures and lives you may not understand very well is misleading and can easily break down into prejudice, even if you don't mean it to. Be who you are, be yourself.

On the subject of your family, a brief digression. I encourage you to tell your children true stories and anecdotes on some evenings. Give them narratives about the great-grandparents, or as far back as you can go. How and when did the family get to America, where did they live here, what did they do to raise their families, earn a living, leave a legacy or a lesson, what were their skills and talents? Your children will feel connected and find a bond with the past that is healthy and natural. Give them a context for their lives with family stories.

But back to naturalness as it applies to imaginative storytelling. Naturalness, your own voice, is one of those things, like imagination, that you lose if you think about it too much. So I won't spend any more time trying to get you to relax and be natural. If someone stands over your shoulder the first time you are going to try to dive into a pool and bellows, "RELAX! RELAX! JUST FALL IN!" you'll probably end up with a belly flop. How much easier it is if that person next to you says quietly, "Go ahead whenever you're ready . . ."

Don't Explain

The story is clipping along, a nice little pace is established and there's a bit of suspense building and all kinds of intriguing signs are appearing and you're really getting into it and all of a sudden you feel the need to explain it so far. "Now, honey, this story is about a little boy just like you who hates having to stay in the yard. The horse with the tall neck that can see over fences is really you. Now, Mommy wants you to stay in the yard, but that doesn't mean that *someday* you won't be old enough to go out on your own. So I am making the horse able to see the field and ready to jump over the fence, because you know that . . ." *Stop!* The story is ruined. You killed it.

Don't interrupt imagination with exposition, with synopsis. If you explain too much, make too many parenthetical remarks, you have taken the child's pleasure and power away. Children take enormous pleasure in stories, if for the sole reason that they are a relief from this sort of blabby factualism which fills their ears from morning to night. The child takes great interest in the fenced-in horse's dilemma and probably knows very well why. There is great security to be gained by having understood one's personal problems and solving them, not in having them explained to us. To always have someone explaining everything is the worst fence there is. Children want to think for themselves. Don't insult your child's intelligence by s-p-e-l-l-i-n-g i-t o-u-t.

I will go even farther with this. If you deny your children the freedom to find meaning for themselves in your stories, you are defeating yourself as well. The price you pay is a bored, indifferent child or, even worse, a child who deeply resents the limits you constantly put on his or her freedom. And what happens then, I think, is that the child preserves this resentment, like a pickle in a jar of vinegar, in the form of self-pity.

Once upon a time, in a very quiet library, there was a small, thin volume whose father was an encyclopedia and whose mother was an unabridged dictionary. Now, this little book had some very nice creamy pages — edged with gold — on which she had made many beautiful line drawings. She had also written in some charming words too, like "bellybutton," "pickle," and "dollop."

But every time this little book started to say something, her father began dropping his volumes with a thud, ruffling noisily through his papers to correct her facts, while the mother had derivations to deliver, and synonyms, and spellings. It made the little book very sorry for herself. She could hardly get a word in edgewise.

One day, she took every one of the corrections they had added to her pages and just tore them out. She tore out the drawings too. She made a little pile of them, right beside her. She got thinner and thinner as the pile got bigger. When the pile was very tall, she sat on it, feeling weak and empty. Her parents did nothing. At last, the little book angrily made a few paper airplanes and threw them at her parents. Her father pulled out his "O" volume and looked up "origami." The mother, however, began to feel anxious.

"What's the matter, trouble, difficulty, all nouns?" she asked.

"I want to think for myself," whispered the little volume.

"What do you need, require, desire, verbs?"

"Freedom and a crayon."

The mother hurried to get her a crayon — it so happens, a red one — and the little book began to write and draw the most wonderful story. She worked feverishly, joyfully, and new pages, dozens of them, grew within her binding. Her parents watched and were quietly relieved and impressed.

"A renaissance, Europe, fourteenth to seventeenth century, my dear," whispered the father.

"Reborn, restored, rejuvenated today," the mother whispered back, smiling.

The little book was happy because she was thicker than ever with pages she had made herself. And the story? Well, someday you'll tell it to me.

◆ The creation of a thousand forests is in one acorn.
— *Ralph Waldo Emerson*

◆ The folk tale is the primer of the picture-language of
the soul.
— *Joseph Campbell*

9

Symbols (Bong) and How to Make Them

◆ ◆ MAKING SYMBOLS is a kind of alchemy. Put in a
Tinkertoy and pull out a bridge that spans the bay; put
in a feather and pull out the good luck of a white bird;
put in a squirt gun and pull out the majestic terror of
Niagara Falls. It's tremendously fun to make symbols,
and very important to the power and depth of your
stories.

Symbols are *objects*, material things, that stand for
bigger concepts, often things you can't touch, such as
thoughts, ideas, emotions, abstractions. The symbol
suggests more than itself. Its economy, its thrift, is

inspiring and at the same time enormously flexible and expressive.

For the purposes of storytelling, it is useful fun to consider some of the intuitively known symbols of world mythology, art, and common usage. They are wonderful inspirations. As you set out to symbolize, to objectify, difficult and complex abstractions in your child's life — intangibles like confusion, hope, power, love, separation — you will find that your stories are more exquisite, powerful, and profound if you can strike the right symbol. *Bong!* I want to give you some ideas about how to approach this pleasure, give you a knack for symbol-making by exploring some of the world's good old standbys, and give you the green light to play with inventing some new ones.

Good Old Standbys

Woods, circle, river, hole, and light are the biggies. There are many other universal symbols too, but these are the ones I have found myself using most often in my stories. They come naturally to me and, I have found, to my children. By two years old, I think, all children have a sort of inchoate understanding of what these old symbols mean. Whether they get the meaning by "blood memory," as the poet Rilke put it, or gain the meaning, like immunities, mysteriously at the breast or in the parent's arms, or simply get "it" from acute observation, you may proceed with confidence that your child will understand general aspects of these symbols when you use them. The classic symbols are an easy way to begin storytelling because they are part of a common "picture-language," as Joseph Campbell calls it. Play with these images.

The Woods

Even if your child has seen only a shadowy grove of ten trees in the park, when you call it a woods, she will get the symbolic meaning of "woods." How uneasy it makes her feel to peer into the snarled growth where there are no easy paths, how confusing and dim it is compared to other places. Every child understands that a deep woods in a story means something very important, scary, confusing.

In your story, the woods has to represent something that is pertinent to your tale and to your child, so don't just plug in a woods and say nothing about it. If you mention a woods, it means something, and your child is waiting for the other shoe to drop. Make the woods a challenge in your story — a place of profound meaning, some of which is tinged with dread — and you'll be neck and neck with the greats. Traditionally the woods represents something difficult and unknown, a horrible place to get lost in. But the beauty of the symbol of the woods, as with all the classic symbols, is that it can stand for so *many* adjacent and conflicting meanings. What does the woods mean in your particular story? It could stand for your hero's confusion about what to do with his problems, the many trees within symbolizing the infinite-seeming number of problems he has. It could stand for a place where wild things might tear him to pieces. Or, in another light, it could stand for the only place in the world where the magic answer can be gained. It could stand for all these at once and more. How you visualize the woods on the night of your story will personalize some of its vast symbolic content, and as you go along, your imagination will add shades of meaning to the wordless given-ness of "woods" that has come from centuries before us.

The woods are a particularly European, American sort of symbol. Probably, if we were living in Egypt, a desert would stand for the same sort of vast wilderness: a place where nature can be indifferent to our sufferings, but where something very important can happen to the hero. The Bible and other great works of literature — among them *The Inferno, Walden,* and even *Robin Hood* — sent their heroes into the wilderness to learn or enact some mighty truth or insight. Somewhere within the woods resides a spirit or a god or an animal or a temptation or an adventure or a hidden secret which provides the hero with guidance, understanding, and growth. The woods are "lovely, dark, and deep," and from them always comes a good thing — a new maturity and confidence in having faced them. Consider the cliché, "You're out of the woods." It is straight from storytelling.

Fairy tales are full of woods as settings for children's difficulties. Nearly everything in "Hansel and Gretel" happens in the woods, from their first abandonment by their woodcutter parents to the final roasting of the witch. Little Red Riding Hood had to cross a woods to get to her grandmother's house and was saved by a woodsman. In "The Wolf and the Seven Little Kids," a mother goat says to her children, "I have to go into the forest, be on your guard against the wolf." Sending the mother figure into the woods is also threatening in stories. In "Brother and Sister," the children left home because their stepmother denied them food, and after a day's walk they came to a large forest and "were so weary with sorrow and hunger . . . that they lay down in a hollow tree and fell asleep." In this story, there was shelter amidst the threat. When Rapunzel was twelve, "the enchantress shut her into a tower which lay in a forest," a place where she would, supposedly, not be found by some prince, but we know better.

And the beat goes on: Stephen Sondheim named his wonderful musical *Into the Woods*; Robert Frost wrote his poem, "Stopping by Woods on a Snowy Evening"; Shakespeare had forests all over the place; Thoreau spent a year on Walden Pond; Toni Morrison, in *Beloved*, created one of the most soaring scenes ever enacted in the woods.

Willa Cather's lovely Ántonia stands in a different sort of woods. We see her in an orchard where she "had only . . . to put her hand on a little crab tree and look up at the apples, to make you feel the goodness of planting and tending and harvesting at last." An orchard is not a tangled, confusing place; its essence is of fruitful cultivation, of orderliness. Have your hero dance in a moonlit orchard in full bloom, or pick the fruit in autumn, or climb the gentle trees, and you'll explore yet another neck of the woods.

Over and over again the image of groves and woods is found in our literature, painting, film, and theater because it is an essential part of our symbolic language. Artists have taken this encompassing symbol of good and evil and made it express something more, something interior, and personal to themselves, as Frost did. You can too.

The Circle

World imagery has been preoccupied with the circle. Perhaps our fascination began with seeing the shape of the mother's breast and nipple — two circles — embodying beauty and survival of the race; or seeing the shape of the sun, feeling its burn upon our shoulders and its effect on all of nature; or seeing the tranquillity of the full moon over the mountains and knowing it soon will wane. Perhaps the circle's greatest moment was when it inspired the discovery of the wheel. It has been with us as long as recorded history, and, I believe, for millenniums before that, symbolizing perfection, bliss, eternity. The circle's circumference is an unending line, a symbol for the continuance of life, or for the repetition of cycles, a line that cannot be escaped, a line that stands for birth and death and ongoing life itself. Religions have grown around it. The solar eye of Horus, in ancient Egypt, was connected in various myths to the sun and the moon. Buddhism has its Wheel of Becoming. Islam sends its pilgrims to walk a circle seven times around a sacred object. Japan has the *yin-yang* circle, with its white fish and black fish curled around each other in a perfect circle, depicting the struggle and resolution of opposites. Stonehenge is the Druids' astonishing calendar, a circle of enormous stone arches surrounded by circular trenches. When dawn rose on the vernal equinox at a specific notch in the circle, they knew the new year had been born.

Earth's orbit is a circle around the sun, which is also a circle. Our Earth rotates on its axis in a circle, as do all the planets and moons. Anything caught in space by the gravity of another object, whirls around it in a circle. Seems the universe is in cahoots with the shape. And down here, clocks, wreaths, rings, halos, mandalas, rose windows, Buddha's thumb and finger, all are in the shape of the circle. Circles are timeless and the measurement of time as well, suggesting outer visions of completion and inner visions of wholeness.

Use a circle in a story; experiment with this classic and see what you get. You will discover that your imagination will expand on what seems a simple symbol. You will express your image of circle, your meaning of circle, and you will find again that your imagination will digress or expand upon the basics. Your hero may have something magical that is a circle: a shield or a Frisbee or a dinner plate. Your hero may be taking actions that are circular and self-defeating, or, like the thorny hedge in "Sleeping Beauty," a circle may enclose and keep your hero safe for a time. Your hero may discover an understanding of life itself from a circular object. As Rumpelstiltskin was able to spin straw into gold with a circular spinning wheel, you too will discover the magic of the circle in the stories you spin.

The River

Jorge Luis Borges said that the only true metaphor of life, the only one worth anything, was "the river of life." The river flows constantly along the banks, never stopping, but every drop is distinct and individual. The river is always the same and always new. You can never step in the same river twice. Put a leaf or a duck in it and it is different and yet still the same. The shimmer of its surface can carry boats loaded with goods, can engulf and drown us, or can inspire us with its beauty, as Monet well knew when he arose at three in the morning to paint his poetic series, *Morning on the Seine.* The river is elemental water, source of life, composite of rain and ground and season. The river is a meeting place for animals and humans alike, a place of life and death. "Ol' Man River" was sung to the Mississippi, and it is a song I suspect Borges would have liked. The river is peace and laziness, flood and drought, delta and tributary. Its source, its beginning, like the rainbow in our myths, is a mystery and a symbol of birth and hope. The river, like humankind, reflects and mirrors what is at its banks, but may, like us, have no idea what those reflections mean. We have heard the river laugh as it runs over pebbles, or roar with destruction at the falls, or murmur in the tender bubbles when we throw our baited line toward a fish. The river feeds, transports, supports crops and livestock, powers engines, cuts chasms in the earth, erodes, and fertilizes. The river washes away dirt, sin, doubt. Cleansing, healing, sustaining, and beautiful, the river runs through our lives and our dreams.

Put a boy and a runaway slave on a raft in the river and suddenly you have the mythic American tale of *Huckleberry Finn.* Carve an Indian in a canoe and set it out on a snow-capped mountain and you have *Paddle-to-the-Sea.* Put Cleopatra on the Nile in a golden boat with silver oars and perfumed sails and you have Shakespeare's evocation of Egypt in all its splendor.

The river is everywhere in our symbolic culture. Rivers mark a boundary, the edge of one thing, the beginning of another. Baby Moses was found in a stream. Jesus was baptized in the River Jordan. Caesar crossed the Rubicon to conquer Pompey; George Washington crossed the Delaware. Throw tea into the harbor and you've got a revolution. The Ganges is holy. The Tigris and Euphrates fork around the birthplace of *Homo sapiens*. We talk about a river of tears, a stream of consciousness, being up a creek or being sold down the river.

The river is so various and evocative of nations, history, and states of mind that as a symbol in your story, I can assure you, it will take you places. Set your hero on a river and see what happens. Make the river his friend or his enemy, and the symbol thrives, because it, like the circle or the woods, is so encompassing. Make the river life itself, and see if you can improve on Borges' remarkable stories of the inner rivers we embody, with our veins and arteries splaying out from and returning to the heart. Oh, go with this one, it is the place of inner tubes and frogs, mosquitoes and herons, salmon and goddesses, water babies and enchantment. If you did nothing but tell river stories, I think you could never exhaust the symbol and the meaning.

The Hole

Call it hell, Hades, a well, a tunnel, a cave, or the underground, the hole is a classic symbol running through our mythology and art since the dawn of human life; it turns out, since the caves. The darkness of the hole is not only of night, but also of primal questions of birth and death. In the hole is something other than life on earth.

To the Greeks, Hades was a gloomy underground where the dead crossed the River Styx and where Persephone lived six months of every year; Homer's Odysseus went down to Hades to find his course to Ithaca, and when he emerged, the next stop was with Polythemus, the Cyclops who lived in a cave.

Give Dante a hole and he writes *The Inferno,* the most mind-boggling study of hell and free will ever written. (He, by the way, also puts in nine circles and four rivers.) Give Shakespeare a cavern and he fills it with witches dancing around a boiling cauldron, mixing the charm on Macbeth. Give Lewis Carroll a rabbit hole and he drops Alice down it into Wonderland, a place of puns, mind games, and transformations, which she can leave only by losing her temper. Tolkien's hobbit hole, on the other hand, is a very pleasant place. "Not a nasty, dirty, wet hole . . . nor yet a dry, bare, sandy hole with nothing in it to sit down on or to eat: it was a hobbit-hole, and that means comfort." Give Mark Twain a cave at the end of *Tom Sawyer* and he hides Injun Joe's treasure in it. Whenever the hero goes into a hole, you can be sure he will emerge with new powers, insights, and rewards.

The hole elicits in us both fear and the desire to explore, probe, ferret in. A cavern caught Leonardo da Vinci's eye one afternoon, and stupefied by the darkness he wrote, "Suddenly there arose in me two things, fear and desire — fear because of the menacing dark cave, and desire to see whether there were any miraculous thing within." These are powerful curiosities in your child today, and the hole symbolizes them perfectly. Use a hole in a bedtime story and your child will know it is a door to enchantment.

Grimm's is full of enchanted holes. In "The Three Feathers," several underground toads (hero-extensions gained by going down into the self) give Simpleton unearthly beautiful things, turn a frog into a princess, a turnip into a horsedrawn coach (forebears of Disney's *Cinderella*). In "Mother Holle," a Persephone figure falls down a well to the realm of Mother Holle, whose featherbed she shakes so well that snow falls on earth. In "Iron Hans" a man-monster found at the bottom of a drained lake becomes an adviser to the hero.

Even cutting-edge science is transfixed with the idea of the hole as a place of burial and birth. A black hole is a dead star that has shrunk to an unimaginable density, the size of a matchbox weighing 260 billion tons, so heavy it sucks even light into it. Some have theorized that black holes are tunnels into other universes!

Tell stories about holes and you will be using the picture-language children understand. Look around you for holes and see what connections they make in your child's life: the hole in a tree could be the safe place for a hero to sleep; the hole dug in a hillside by a ground hog or a coyote could start you off on wonderful new characters; the hole that's left when a tree falls in a storm could be the inspiration for stories about the mushroom kingdom. Or how about the hole your child digs to China? Tell stories about holes and you will dig up something wonderful.

Light

Light symbolizes a tremendous number of good things in our world: birth, intelligence, heaven, love, truth, triumph, joy, and life itself. Light is a flame, a fire, an answer, a skill, a passion. We see a beautiful light in the eyes of a loved one. We don't want to hide our light under a bushel. We talk about sweetness and light, the light of perfection. When we love someone, they are the light of our life. "But soft? What light through yonder window breaks?" We, like Dylan Thomas, "rage, rage at the dying of the light." We look for it at the end of the tunnel; we put one in the window. We talk about the light of reason, the light of understanding. We've named a whole period of history the Enlightenment. Bacon said God's first creature was light. We paddle down the river "By the Light of the Silvery Moon." Lightning makes us wince. Light is the key to Einstein's formula, $E = mc^2$. The Impressionists painted it, poets praise it, people can go crazy without it. Light has entered our symbolic language to such a degree that it is nearly blinding.

Play with it in your stories. Fairyland is full of light. Give your character a light of some kind and your child instinctively understands that that character is important and has a power. A lantern in your story, a jacket of light, a crown of light, a light shining on the top of a mountain, a flashlight, all communicate something de-*light*-ful. Give your hero light, or make him seek something that is shining, or bring him home to a houseful of light, or, better yet, escort him home with thousands of fireflies, and your stories will be filled with magic. Light is hope. It is a vast symbol; it never goes out.

A Grab Bag of Familiar Symbols

The *witch* is such an ancient symbol of evil that I need hardly go much further. But if you, like I, get a bit weary of making a female figure be the personification of evil, try a *goblin* or a *warlock* for a male figure. Remember, telling a story about a witch or a goblin is a serious matter, one that you should not take lightly. Children somehow know that a witch is deadly magic because she is more than mortal. And you'd better be ready to deal as violently with her as she is with your hero.

There are scores of stock symbols for you to choose from in our great picture-language. Here are some of the most prominent. The *tree* is a source of food and fuel and a safe harbor for children lost in the woods or threatened by beasts. It has *roots*, like family roots, that connect with the earth. It is home to *birds*, who are plucky, far-seeing creatures, message carriers, good omens. Nearby may be the *fox*, a cunning creature, the bearer of good advice, almost like an uncle in most traditional tales. The fox can seat the hero on his tail and run so fast that "hair whistles in the wind." He has a cousin, the *coyote*, who takes on similar tones of wily good sense but is a loner. And of course, the *wolf* is always a bad guy, devouring, tricking, deceiving.

The *white bird* is almost like an *angel* in stories, especially if it appears right after the threat. The white bird or dove goes all the way back to Egypt for symbolic power, and it often represents the superego, the conscience of the tale. The *rock* is the symbol of the loss of human feeling, of paralysis or living death. If the hero is changed into a rock, you've said something very troubling to a child. It is a punishment in fairy tales, often given to the older siblings or competitors of the hero who fail in some task, and often the hero later brings them back to life. The *frog* is really the prince, making the young heroine squeamish with his dank, wrinkled skin. The frog is often a sexual symbol and cannot be truly loved in his "animal" form. Frogs, however, sing in ponds, can live underground, and once these amphibians are shown what's what (as in "The Frog-King," thrown against a wall in anger by the little girl and landing as a gorgeous man), can be transformed or work magic. There are other animal grooms in fairy tales — *hedgehogs* and *bears*, for instance — who are made lovable only by being loved. Large birds like *ravens* and *swans* and beautiful animals like *deer* are often brothers under enchantment. *Ants* are industrious little hero substitutes, as are *fish*, *ducks*, and *honeybees*.

Seeds in fairy tales are scattered around as symbols of the details that must be mastered in a task, to be picked up in one night by the hero. *Golden anythings* are magic, straight out. Golden flowers, birds, cages, rooms, have an otherworldly quality, beyond the never-never land. They seem to have taken form in an unfathomable past time. *Giants* are parents made stupid and cruel, as are *dragons* and *witches*, who take cruelty to evil levels. *Dwarfs* are limited men, symbols of adolescence, and are sometimes good, as in "Snow White," and sometimes nasty, as in "Snow White and

Rose Red." To fall into *sleep* for a hundred years or to be put in a glass coffin under enchantment are symbolic ways of talking about adolescence, when everything seems to go inside to be awakened at a later time. *Speechlessness,* long periods of *servitude,* or being put in a *tower* and kept from the world are also symbols of adolescence.

The number *three* is important in traditional fairy tales. It is used in many ways, but most often the hero is given three chances to wise up about a problem. Three brothers or three pigs often confront the same dilemma in a story, and only the youngest one figures it out. Or there are three trials that the hero must solve to finally win the kingdom. *Kingdoms* mean adulthood, symbolizing the power to make one's own independent decisions and to live wisely; *marriage* symbolizes the end of loneliness, of the search, and of separation from parents. These are the tip of the iceberg.

How to Find the Right Symbol: The Far-seeing Eye

Wilhelm Grimm wrote that fairy tales contain "fragments of belief dating back to most ancient times, in which spiritual things are expressed in a figurative manner." And then he went on to make a beautiful metaphor of the value of storytelling by saying that "the mythic element resembles small pieces of a shattered jewel which are lying strewn on the ground, all over-grown with grass and flowers, and only can be discovered by the most far-seeing eye."

You can be that most far-seeing eye by discovering

the right symbols for your stories. There is something at once simple and mysterious about the process of doing this. The simple part is this: look around. Right in your child's room are dozens, perhaps hundreds, of objects that can become symbolic of immaterial things and can come to signify ideas and concerns of your child. The magic of storytelling involves the use of the ordinary in extraordinary ways. For instance, a backpack, a book, a flashlight, or a blanket each carries a symbolic content you can readily use in a story by extending it, exaggerating it, giving it an enchanted air. An extraordinary book could stand for the power of learning, a flashlight for the penetrating power of focused attention, a blanket for the sweetness of home. I like using children's possessions as positive symbols because it brings the symbolic power closer to the child and makes it an extension of the child. The magic backpack has more attachment for the listening child than does the mother's purse or the father's billfold. The backpack could symbolize the portability of knowledge, while the billfold becomes an object symbolizing the abstraction of money or credit. A purse contains these as well as personal items, and could symbolize any number of things about the mother. A backpack usually has no implication of money at all. The ownership of the magic symbol attaches the power to that owner. If you wish to make a magic object of one of your possessions, that's fine too. Just realize that since it is yours, the story then involves some of your power. The magic ball of yarn, for instance, may be a great way not to get lost in the woods, but it implies the power of the knitter.

The mysterious part of symbol creation, the part

that springs out at you from the bushes of your imagination, is that although you may *think* you know what the yo-yo, the backpack, or the daisy crown is going to symbolize, you find that, as the story goes on, more information will arise as to the meaning. The daisy crown may start out as a symbol of sweet girlish innocence, all flower-round and lovely, a powerful circle, but as you go along you discover that in your story it begins to mean disillusionment as it flops and wilts. You keep going, and you come to the idea that as daisies wilt, they scatter their seeds wherever the girl walks, making her a sort of female Johnny Appleseed. Any symbol has many meanings: do not be afraid to follow where the story leads you within the pattern I have already described. This multiplicity of meanings is part of the fun, an essential part of the discovery of storytelling. This is the far-seeing eye.

So often it is the magic of *meaning* itself that attempts to communicate with us by way of our imaginations. We find as we listen to its whispers that new insights and understandings surface, that suddenly there is a quality — about daisy crowns, for instance — that has eluded us all these years. Indeed, the girlish crown has become magic because we have learned something touching, affecting, thought-provoking from it. And so, as you tell stories, you become an explorer and guardian of the eternal symbols, and a source of beauty, growth, and understanding for your child.

Start with an Object

Imagine yourself in the child's room and you are, for the moment, empty-headed, uninspired, a blob with not the slightest idea of what to tell a story about. Scan the room for an object that interests you. It can be anything — jacks, a ball, a sweater, a piece of string. If you pause for a moment, if you play the game of association with yourself, you will find your story for the night. Jacks may start you out thinking about a rhyme you once said as you played the game. Use it in your story and create a tale around it. The ball is the circle, so associate on that one, make the ball magic in the story, make it a ball that always comes back to the thrower, or a ball that can find things in the playground, or a ball that is so heavy no one could pick it up. A sweater is warm and fuzzy; make it a magic sweater and make it do something that you believe in. Perhaps it symbolizes for you the warmth of the world, and your story can go out from the object into a tale about children or people who are cold. If the string catches your eye, just toy with the idea of string and your imagination will give you a lead on your story.

Fitting the Symbol into Your Story

The symbol can fit into any of the five parts of your story. (1) There was a likable hero (2) who had reason to set out on a journey (3) when a threat occurred (4) from which there was a hero-inspired way out (5) which resulted in a safe return and a happy ending.

Plug the symbolic object into one of the five parts of the story, and see where it leads. Take the string as an example. (1) As a hero: The poor little string could be the unattached hero looking for a yo-yo; or the string could be the naughty shoelace that loves to come untied. The hero-string could be the one that has nothing to do and is pent-up and useless until the day of the kite-flying contest. (2) As motivation: The string could have a glittering end that is sitting on the hero's doorstep one morning and then trails off, mysteriously, down the hill. The string could be tied up in hard knots and come to the hero for help. (3) As threat: The string could be the bad guy, a horrible, tangled, sticky wad that tries to tie the hero up, or blocks her escape, or is strung on a loom she must walk over. (4) As escape: The string could be the solution to the hero's problem, at the crucial moment, pulled off her ponytail or whisked out of her pocket or shoe to tie the rat's legs up, or keep her boat from floating away. (5) As a reward at the happy ending: The string could be the thing you use at the end of the story that brings your hero to the safety of home. Your hero is happy to find everything just as she left it on her shelf: her books, her toys, and, best of all, that irreplaceable piece of string that was once attached to her birthday balloon.

Let yourself go with it. Fly! Plug the ordinary object into one of the five parts of the story and you have endless variations before you.

Transformation and Ambiguity

Of course, symbols are as common as sense, as plentiful as nouns in the language. I suppose *any* object can be a symbol if you apply your imagination to it, and in the same way any dilemma, emotion, threat, or reward can be symbolized. The trick is to make the match. A rule of thumb in storytelling is to go with whatever has the highest rank in your child's life, or yours, that day. What sticks out? If it was an experience, then you've got to find an object or environment to stand for it; and I think the old standbys will serve you well here and cover a lot of bases. If it was the sight of a fascinating new thing, let that thing symbolize some interesting idea, and then go ahead and build a story. One fact about inventing stories is that you don't have a lot of time to weigh things out, make delicate, time-consuming comparisons. Something jumps out at you in the equation, and you just have to make up the other side. It's kind of a game of association, and I can tell you, it is great fun.

When I start a story, I like to think of symbolic things that change and become better through transformation. This is, after all, what I'm trying to tell my child about his or her life. Certainly the great standbys are capable of nearly infinite change, the woods, the circle, the river, the hole, and light. But there are hundreds of little specific objects around home — like popcorn, melting butter, ice cubes — that can change too. Transformation is a wondrous part of childhood. Seeds become plants, caterpillars become butterflies, children become adults. Make them a part of your story and let them have their changes. It's the Ugly Duckling pattern. Your child will understand and learn; and you will have the fun of being the maker of alchemies, the discoverer of the beautiful changes around you.

As a rule, symbols are not ambiguous in bedtime stories. The evil witch does not have a good quality that softens our hatred of her. The bird on the bough does not befoul Cinderella's hazel tree. The hole is not both good and bad. The river is not good and bad at the same time. Symbols have to stand for something that is simple and unambiguous. If you make a story rich in symbols, do not try to make them have the gray tones that we adults so appreciate. It is too complicated for a bedtime story and, I believe, not as engaging, let alone instructive, for the child to have to try to figure out if this is a good apple or a bad one. Take a stand on your symbol for the night and don't clutter it up with too many conflicting meanings. If you feel that rivers or holes or apples can go both ways, that's fine, I agree with you, but tell one side of the story at a time. Polarization is a large part of the child's mind, and by sticking with it, you will build a better story.

Now, this doesn't mean that within your scary forest there cannot be a kindly tree. Or that under the raging current of a river there doesn't live a calm and courageous rainbow trout. To the contrary. Within your encompassing symbol, you are really and truly free to seek those subplots and characters who will do your hero good.

If you feel strongly about the importance of shades of meaning, about ambiguity as a reality in life, I agree again. There is a way to involve our subtle understandings in storytelling by doing a medley of stories using the same symbol again and again, varying it each night. One night the apple is from the tree of life and is all good and fills the world with apple pie or apple cider. The next night it has been poisoned by a witch and is therefore not to be eaten. The next night it could be a hardhearted apple that cannot be cut in two by any knife but when put on the ground is broken by the rain, which exposes its inner seed to earth, and it becomes the first tree in an orchard, softened by its contact with nature, reformed by its acquaintance with rain. Next night it is another apple: a computer, or the apple of someone's eye, or the Adam's apple in the hero's throat that helps him sing. Doing the medley on apples, you can express the ambiguousness of your symbol, and your child will begin to see how many ways it feeds, sustains, and symbolizes life. We can continue the great myth of the Garden of Eden, tasting the apple from the Tree of Knowledge of Good and Evil . . . but one bite at a time, please. Let us not choke our children with too much convoluted symbolism. It isn't good for them, I think, and more important, it is very hard for you as a storyteller to do. You simply lose track of your meaning and get confused and distracted and lost and suddenly all your apple means is confusion and muddle and sauce.

Free Reign, Free Rein, Free Rain

Any noun can become a radiating star of meaning. Any object can stand for something else, as words themselves do. Let yourself go, be free, experimental, open-minded, even silly. Don't censure your little quiet thoughts; let them come to you. You are the good king or queen in the land of imagination, so give yourself free reign to see the farthest, smallest, most hidden parts of your kingdom; there is nothing to restrict your power, for in fact you are — temporarily — omniscient. Somewhere, far away, under the flowers and grass, is a shattered jewel. Seek it on the whitest, fastest horse in the world and give him free reins, give him his head. Let your sensory impressions lead in you as you ride in search of symbols that fill the mind. And let nature, the weathers and seasons, pour down on you as you go. Let the raindrops be felt on your face and each drop free to run down the way it will. There is magic in these reigns, reins, rains.

◆ If we do not hope for peace we cannot find it.
 — *Elie Wiesel*

10

Happy Endings

◆ ◆ AND SO Hansel and Gretel were devoured by the witch; and so the weasel won and the bunny's parents never got over it; and so the wolf went home with his stomach bulging and slept it off; and so the youth failed to pick up all the seeds and was sent to his death in the waves; and so the couple never met again and wandered the earth in blindness until their early, solitary deaths.

How d'ya like them apples? I don't. I think a nihilistic, cynical, tragic ending to any bedtime story is destructive. I don't enjoy Hans Christian Andersen's "The Little Fir Tree," in which a pitiful young pine tree is cut away from its family forest, decorated with lights and candles for a couple of brief shining days and then stripped, left standing forgotten in a corner of the attic to wilt and lose its needles and finally be burned. It must have been fashionable then to tell such fantasy to children. What cruel fashion! Cautionary tales warned children that their thumbs would fall off if they sucked them. Hateful stories. No wonder so many parents turned away completely from fairy tales, thinking them all as bad as these cheap imitations. The cruel ending, however, is still with us. *The Giving Tree* is a recent tragedy written for little children. In it a boy swings on an apple tree who gives and gives to him, but as he grows, he forgets the bounty and beauty of the tree, begins to take advantage of its generosity, and, in stages, cuts it down. And the tree lets him do it! At last he is an old man, has killed the tree and sits on its stump facing with blank eyes his own death. Too late — he should have died young. I am against tragic endings for children because they are defenseless; their lives have not been long enough to contemplate tragedy appropriately.

Labels Stick

Because children tend to live up to what we expect of them and of life, our labels stick. When I overhear a parent berating a child as a "stupid brat," I am tempted to intrude and say, "If there is one way to create a 'stupid brat,' that's *it*." I feel sorry for the child, because I believe that children are very sincerely trying to prove to us how *worthy* they are of our love and protection. Their main worry is that we do not find them worthy enough. If we tell them they don't deserve our care, they'll live up to it.

In the same way, what you ascribe to the hero in your story applies to your listening child too. If your hero is a failure and a klutz and a fool to the bitter end of the story, your child will get a very negative message from it. Furthermore, the story that ends unhappily does nothing to free the child from any preoccupations or fears, any ignorance or loneliness, any puzzlement or frustration. It does nothing to build a courageous spirit or a willingness to let go of infantile things. It does not inform or encourage but rather keeps children in a muddle of worry about the sadness, the defeat, of the ending, turning it over and over in their minds, never letting them out of the cage of childishness. The tragic ending does not reward at all; rather, it is a sort of psychological punishment. If you cannot imagine a happy ending to your stories, don't tell them. Read Grimm's fairy tales aloud.

The Moral Heart of the Happy Ending

The storyteller has a crucial choice to make at the end of a story. The question is: which is more important, the child or the problem? In other words, for all of us the question is: what is more eternal, our humanness or the forces of chaos?

The unhappy ending basically tells children that the problem is more important than he is; that chaos cannot be mastered by our human efforts. Hazard, pain, and stuckness are more powerful than facing the difficulty, struggling with it, learning from it, and moving on. If all of us thought that problems were more important than people, we would still be grunting in caves instead of flying airplanes, inventing vaccines, and writing operas. Allowing a problem to overwhelm the hero in your story is to say that there's really no use in trying; why go on, why stretch, risk, reach, why think, love, or do anything? This is the stuff of future horrors for the individual child and for society.

We need a kind of learned, moral optimism, I believe. *Which* morals is up to the family, up to you. Although bedtime stories are certainly not the answer to society's ills, they *do* share — on the special individual, imaginary, emotional level — what *you* have learned about worthiness, pluck, accomplishment, gumption, self-esteem, goodness, meaning, and even perhaps "the rapture of being alive." Your stories show your child that you've given some thought to this path, this woods, and that you believe there are some tricks to it, some techniques worth knowing, some tools worth having. And you give them to your child. Also, as you tell your stories, you affirm that there is wisdom and pleasure to be gained from one's family. I urge you to share with your child those values you believe will enhance his or her life. As you do so, you will strengthen your child and the family bonds. And most important, your child deeply wants to know.

Bring the morals and virtues you hold dear into your stories by following the structure I have outlined above, and end the story happily. This is not a cinch, and shouldn't be pat or banal. It takes effort and imagination, but you can do it. My moral code, as you may have gathered so far, revolves around loving relationships and communication, so my happy endings often bring the peace of friendship strengthened, the peace of knowing one is loved, the dignity that is gained, not by dire battle, but by generosity, cooperation, or unselfishness.

Your happy ending demands some opinion, belief, and reflection from you. You are searching for a life-affirming note at the end of the story, a human victory of some kind. Every night, you will find one if you look for it. I believe this effort will help your child in the lifelong task of maturation. I *know* it can help you feel you are giving your child a profound form of your love and experience. He or she will translate the ending into real life one way or another. With an accumulation of happy endings, your child will try to meet hardships in real life with enough self-confidence to strive to win over them. And imagination is the source of it. It is a wonder and a joy that this works!

My job as a parent is to hope for my children. I think it is contagious. My hope (I hope) gives them courage to be their best. Courage is, in fact, the inside, the guts, of growth. And we all need it. It requires courage for me to invent happy endings because I don't know all the final answers. I have to act, love, think, and create as best I can, even if I turn out to be wrong. But in doing so, I am searching and growing too.

I can give my children all kinds of bad advice, make all kinds of well-meaning mistakes, even go so far as to tell crummy, boring stories, and they will survive them. But my child cannot be expected to thrive if I lose hope and courage. My happy ending says that I believe *my* life is worth living (partly because I have children), that I believe we all can find meaning in life,

feel the thrill of being here, if we courageously, hope-
fully persevere with what we value. I think that these
are "true" endings, the human, living ones.

Make the Ending Unequivocal

Since children see the world in extremes, without the
gray shadings of adulthood, your stories should be unequivocal about the meaning gained at the end of a
struggle. Now you may be saying to yourself that happiness is never whole, one hundred percent, so why
should you say it is? My answer is yes, that's true, but
children are too early in their development to understand a sixty/forty portion of happiness/unhappiness
contained in one story. Children cannot take the veri-
similitude, the mixed bag of insights that we appreciate
in our adult art forms because children have few ways
of knowing the other side of the story. They don't
experience mixed emotions very often. They see things
wholly, all this or all that. If they don't like radishes,
nothing can redeem them. If they like mud, they will
not be dissuaded from playing in it, even though they
may pretend to avoid it for your sake. They are little
extremists.

When you see a tragic movie or play or horrendous
newsclip, there are actions you can take in response to
your feeling. You can do some small thing about tragedy: offer support, food, money, your help. Children
can't. They are more powerless than you are to do
anything about the world situation, starvation, war,
poverty, disease, and suffering. Day after day, children
experience disappointment and failure. They can't

reach it, they can't open it, they can't drive it, they can't buy it, they can't go wherever they want to. Sometimes their only power is in refusal, refusal to eat something, refusal to be quiet, refusal to use the bathroom, refusal to do their homework — whatever you want at the time, they don't. Imagine that *your* only power were refusal. I think we've got to give them the happy ending.

The unequivocal ending is important too because children have a different sense of time than we do. After a disappointment, most of us could stand to wait a year, say, for another crack at it. But in their brief lifetimes, a day is a long time, and a month is forever. "Someday, honey, thirteen years from now, you will be able to drive a car" is not very consoling, but a story about a mouse who can fly on an eagle's back is. The eagle is you, by the way, giving your child a thrilling ride. Don't forget this. Give your children time to gain the confidence they need to confront their problems. Give them time to outgrow the extremist mentality they have. Give them clear-cut happy endings that help them see that time can be shortened, imaginatively, to the day when they have more maturity, independence, and knowledge.

Providing a Balanced View of Life

Some parents worry that they are giving their child a false and sentimental view of life by always providing the happy ending. They say things like, "I don't want my child to think that the world is a goody-goody place where happiness is forevermore. That's unrealistic."

My answer is that children know this already. A bedtime story is not a total view of life but a glance at one part of it. A bedtime story is "once upon a time." Children know that the story is not meant to represent life as it is exactly lived, real, concrete, right-now life on the outside. Rather, they understand that this is the land of make-believe and that all is spoken in a picture-language. Your stories are about life on the inside, within the emotions and thoughts, in an imaginary land, and about a specific problem. In this context, a happy ending is very realistic.

And too, as one night's story ends happily, what happens the next night and the next? More difficulties arise in your stories, just as they do in your child's life. Every night the promised happiness is again challenged and seems for the moment tenuous. Every night there is a new threat, another obstacle, another setback that informs the child that life is not a bowl of cherries by any means. Your nightly stories accumulate to tell the truth — that life is full of difficulties — yet, one at a time, these difficulties can be overcome and some meaning can be wrung from them. And the other shining truth also emerges: life is full of small accomplishments, miraculous escapes, joyful reunions, treasures, and rewards. The accumulation of your stories will bring a balanced view of life.

Marriage as a Symbolic Happy Ending

I want to defend the symbol of marriage as a happy ending and encourage you to use this symbol from time to time. If your hero is an animal, of course, it is ridiculous to put the mouse in a tuxedo or veil and march it down the aisle as some sort of payoff for jumping on the button at the car wash. The symbol of marriage is not the reward for overcoming infantile fears and childish ignorance; there are many more stages to be gone through before the promise of a loving partner is a really valid part of a child's concerns.

But when you sense that it is becoming a part of your child's concerns, tell stories that end with your hero finding a long-term companion. Marriage is a *symbol* of this which children readily understand. As in fairy tales, your human heroes may have endured long symbolic trials in the story — years of wandering, chores for a bunch of work-obsessed dwarfs, memorizing the telephone book — but at the end of that period of isolation and challenge, also known as adolescence, a marriage ending is appropriate. It symbolizes adulthood and a loving relationship.

The idea of this adult relationship is consoling to your child, who has a fear of separation from you. If there is nothing more dreadful to a child than being abandoned, there is also nothing more reassuring than the idea that with adulthood we will not be alone but rather living with a loved one.

In order to find that person, the story says, some trials must be endured and some lessons learned. A failed relationship in the real world doesn't mean that the desire for a partner is cornball, naïve, or deluded. There is a yearning in all of us for the right one, for another loved one, a partner sometime later in life — a beloved — who will take the ache out of being grown and alone and separate. The wish to live contentedly with a true partner still flourishes in the hearts of both children and adults.

If you know what works for your successful relationship, describe it symbolically in a story. For me, I would say both people have to be determined to make it work; understanding and forgiveness are useful; some kind of mutual support or shared passion is necessary; and both must have a willingness to amend their definition of love. As you create an ending to your story, remember that this is not an excuse to blurt your confusions but rather a time to convey and explore more fully what you value. There is value in reticence. If you're disappointed with the term "marriage," create an alternative your child will understand as a tender, fulfilling life with another person, one that can replace the life you share now. I like to call it marriage.

The Problem of Death

Of course, a happy ending is unrealistic in one sense. As a friend of mine once said, with a cowboy twang in her voice, "We're none of us goin' to git out of this thang alive." There is an end to life; death is inevitable. Children realize this at a young age, and it is as difficult for them to understand as it is for us. Perhaps more so. I want you never to end a story with the death of the hero, but there are times when you may need to talk to your child about the fact of the death of a relative, friend, or family pet. Storytelling is a deeply satisfying way to do this. Simply talking and listening to and touching your child is the first thing you must do, of course, but if you wish to address the subject of death using a bedtime story, to discuss the loss on an imaginary level, I think it is a very good idea. Making a story about loss and grief is just as valid as addressing any other situation or emotion in your child's life. What you must *not* do, however, is to end the story with the death. You must make the death happen in the third part, the threat section of the story, and spend the rest of the tale expressing symbolically what you believe happens after death to the loved one and to the living. Stories are about resolutions to problems, not the problems alone.

Since none of us have the final answers, we must do the best we can. If you are bereaved along with your child, this moment will call up your courage and heart as never before. You must make do with what you know and believe, and trust that it will be sufficient. Search your heart, as you probably already have done, to find what religious, spiritual response you truthfully believe is the best way to explain to your child what happens after death. It may entail what you believe happens to the person who has died, as well as what you believe the task of the living is after loss. How do we get through the sorrow of loss, and what must we do to honor and remember the loved one? Take what you believe as your guide, follow your heart, for it is always the best way, limited and finite though it is.

This is how I would handle it. Create a story that has a hero like your child, and then create a symbolic "other" for the loved one who has died. I would not have the other character be the exact person or animal that you and your child have lost, but someone who has some of the make-up, some of the traits, of the loved one. Set them out on their journey together. Do not be afraid of your own imagination here. I urge you to trust it still, even as you know that this "other" must die soon in your story; let your imagination give you comfort and insights as it will. Fine and powerful ideas come from profound feeling; let them come to you, for you are an artist now, creating another important story.

Complete the first two sections of the tale. In the third section, have the "other" character die in a similar way to the actual death, be it long and hard, be it quick and merciful, be it violent or in sleep. I would make the death a bit different in detail than the actual one; I would give it some distance but would maintain some true aspects of it. Do this in the third part of the story, just as you would handle the threat section. Tailor it, as you always do, to your child's personality and level of understanding, but do not babify it, for now more than ever you want to encourage your child to reach in his or her understanding. Tailor the death to match what you believe is best for your child to know. Definitely deal with what the child has seen, heard, and felt about the death. You must address what your child has actually experienced, but you do not have to reveal all you know. Hold back, be gentle, be benevolent, but do not pussyfoot with your child's awareness — children often know and understand more than you think.

This third section is where any horror or pain or anger or fright belongs, where any difficulty and shock is registered and described. Once this section of the story is complete, you must leave these hard, sad, frightening aspects behind and come into the resolution of your story with a sense of the beliefs and attitudes you wish to give your child.

Put your belief into the fourth section of your story, where the hero escapes the threat and resolves it. If you believe that there is a heaven, this is where you must describe it, explain it, populate it. If you believe that there is a soul, here is where it is freed from the body, incorporated into something else, the air, the wind, the sea, some vast holding place for beauty and love. Follow the soul, not the body, in the story. Have the hero (your child) stay behind; I don't believe that children really want to go with the dead one, but they want to know where the loved one has gone. Tell them what you believe, inadequate and bereaved though it may be; tell them as much as you know.

Keep your heart and imagination on the hero in this fourth part of your story, for the hero is your child, trying to come to terms with the separation. The hero is now you as well. Offer your belief, give it as a love gift to your child. Put it symbolically if you can, or just do your best with words. Have the hero muse and talk to himself, have the hero be told wise things by a wise figure, a hero-extension, have the hero find something on which the message is written; there are many ways to give the idea. You'll find the right one. Or just say, "The hero wanted to ask God to change this fact, but he knew that wish could not be granted. Nothing could change the fact that the 'other' was dead. So he asked God for the strength to endure the sorrow and find ways to accept it, and that was granted. The hero could almost feel this strength move into him like a mysterious, silent breath."

If you do not believe in heaven and soul and God,

then you must still imagine a way to console your child. Let the "other" go back to nature, to the earth, to the grasses, to the winds and fields, into the songs of birds, into the voices of dreams — whatever comes to you is worthy, if it is tenderly aimed at your child.

Once upon a time, high in the green mountains, there was an old man who spent his days in a garden beside his home. He ate rich soups and sweet pies and sometimes gave food away. While he tended the garden, he would think of many things, and often about his grandson.

Now this old man had a magic laugh that not everybody could hear. But when they were together, the boy could hear it. Whenever the old man laughed, softly and so deep, everything the boy looked at would speak to him. The boy could hear the seeds saying, "Tuck me in," and the apple trees calling, "Climb us." When they walked to a secret spring deep in the woods, and the boy filled the bottle to overflowing, the old man laughed. And the spring said to the boy, "Where have you been so long? I've missed you."

One day the boy's mother told him the old man was dead. The boy couldn't believe it. "No!" he cried, again and again, and went outside and tried to understand. He ran to his grandfather's house. It was so quiet all around as the snow fell that he began to cry. The garden was broken and silent. He walked to the apple trees and listened. Nothing. At last he came to the spring, which flowed clean and cold, as always, but the magic had left it.

And then the boy remembered the old man's laugh, how it entered the quiet and made things different. He leaned over the spring and felt its foggy breath against his cheek. He tipped his head under the cold water, and it ran all over his face till even the tears were cold. He drank a little.

And then he did a strange thing. He laughed. Not a happy laugh, but a deep, remembering one. Like the old man's. The spring said, "Whenever you feel sad, remember his laugh and how he loved you. Love like that doesn't die. Now it's inside you."

When he went home, he was very tired. His mother touched his hand. "I went to the spring," said the boy. "And I remembered his laugh. I'm sure he wants me to have it. And so I do." And the boy did such a fine imitation that both of them laughed and hugged each other and looked for a long time into each other's eyes.

The basic decency of stories for your children requires that you express something positive to be gained from this loss. You must finish your story with this in mind. Perhaps the qualities of the person who has died live on in some way in your child and hero, perhaps some good work or acts of kindness shown during the lifetime of the deceased continue to reverberate in the land of the living.

Remember as you reach the end of the story that vivid suffering is over. This is the consoling finish. Remember that you are telling your child what you believe is worth knowing for his or her grief and well-being. Keep in mind that your child is very much alive and very human. You will discover that you are too, and that you will be comforted as well.

As the story returns the hero to the real world again, you will both feel what Dante expressed at the end of *The Inferno* as the poet emerged from the blackness of hell: "And so we came forth, and once again beheld the stars." There still remains, in the real world, shared and compassionate emotion. People live on who love each other and who will remember together. The hero, the child, is not alone at the end of the story; he has a valuable gift of love to hold against the twilight of the gods. It is something that you have given him.

Sudden Joyous Turns

J. R. R. Tolkien, the author of *The Lord of the Rings,* describes the facets necessary in a good fairy tale as fantasy, recovery, escape, and consolation. Speaking of the happy ending, Tolkien stresses that all complete fairy stories must have it. It is "a sudden joyous 'turn' . . . however fantastic or terrible the adventure, it can give the child or man that hears it, when the 'turn' comes, a catch of breath, a beat and lifting of the heart, near to tears."

The consolation of the happy ending that you give your child at the end of an adventure could be an infinite number of things. It could be a treasure, new power, an extra inch at the end of his fingertips, or his own sweet home; it could be strawberries on the path, or a gold medal, a new baseball bat, a ride in a balloon, or a clean white bed, perfect for a good night's sleep. The point of the happy ending is to appropriately console the listener for the sorrow and fear of the earlier parts of the story with the welcome news, the vicarious victory, that something fine has come from the sad struggle. The ultimate consolation, one you will use occasionally, is that the hero will not be alone.

♦ I believe the power of observation in numbers of very
young children to be quite wonderful for its closeness
and accuracy . . . Grown men who are remarkable
in this respect may . . . be said not to have lost the
faculty . . . Such men retain a certain freshness,
and gentleness, and capacity of being pleased, which
are also an inheritance they have preserved from
their childhood.
— *Charles Dickens*

11

Gathering In
the Sparks

♦ ♦ HERE'S MY LAST SECRET. The way to tell really good
stories is to open your eyes upon the world, to look at
it intentionally — sensitively observe, gaze, watch,
and study it. Cultivate an attitude of seeing. As you do
so, you will gather innumerable sparks, reflections, and
images that nourish your whole being. Use your inner
binoculars and inner magnifying glass upon the world,
and what you gather will be unconsciously loaded into
your story bin.

Take Nature

Your stories will have expressive settings, ringing symbols, thunderous excitement, and peaceful endings if you try to observe nature and bring it, and what you learn from it, into your stories. In nature — seasons, water, air, animals, the whole miraculous earth — you will find infinite story material. You will never exhaust its inspiration.

Because you have a child, you have an enviable role model in your life; nothing is ordinary, mundane, expected, banal to your youngster. Approach it as your child does and as the child you once were. There was a point, long ago in your life, when everything was new to you, when nothing had a *name*. I try to imagine what it must have been like. How like a kind of insanity it must have been to have never seen, for instance, this nameless thing — this snow — and suddenly find the whole air whirling with it, without even the word "unreal" to describe it. To catch a flake on a fingertip and see it transformed to a pinpoint of water! Can everything do this? If so, what about me? Children want to know these things and crave the understandings we take for granted. I try to feel a child's delight, the child's "aha!" in order to gather material for stories. As with creativity, you have to *want to* before it happens. Cultivate this perspective in yourself.

But you may be saying, "I live in a big city and I'm not so sure I want to be *that* observant. It's ugly out there." I understand. I think people in cities *have* lost what Gretel Ehrlich called "the solace of open spaces."

It is easy to thrill from a mountaintop or gaze with awe at the Pacific, but the city is difficult. Sometimes you don't want to look at where you are; the paved land, the litter, the grime, the ugliness stops you. On the other hand, there is magnificence to be seen in the city's architecture, history in a cornice, delight in the green curves, the slanting tops, the castle battlements of our newest buildings; you need only to look up to see them. I grant that the clutter of cities, the disappointment within them, and the absence of nature's sweeping scale is a great obstacle to seeing; you sometimes choose to shut down your perceptions, but if you are not really *trying* to see, your stories are going to be flat.

So I say, choose to look at something that doesn't depress you. Make it a point to go outside every day to observe, freshly, some plain old ordinary thing or, better yet, something you haven't noticed before. I believe that most of the time you will enjoy what you discover, and most assuredly will be enriched by your *intention* to see. It is possible to get a dose of nature, every day, even in Manhattan. On the most urban street where garbage bags seep fluids onto the sidewalk, pedestrians jam past you, and traffic honks, you can choose where you spend your vision. Stop for a moment and notice the migratory clouds, a steadfast plant, a transcendent bird. As Blake said, "How do you know but every Bird that cuts the airy way, / is an immense world of delight . . ." You don't know till you look for it. Get in as close as you can and purposely look for fresh details. The dandelion by the bus stop has something magnificent to say about survival and bloom, or a hundred other things that might occur to you as you gaze at it.

James Russell Lowell said, "A weed is nothing more than a flower in disguise." Could you draw it from memory? Study how zap-yellow it is, how its squared-off petals radiate out of an almost hairlike center. If you saw one done in gold and emeralds, twenty times life-size, in an Egyptian museum, you'd take a moment. Consider the white globe of ingenious seeds ready to float away with one puff.

As your child would, stop at a pool of broken glass, glittering and turquoise, on the sidewalk; pick up a piece and see the imperfections inside, the dust motes, like stars. Or go to the park and look at the grass, at the crease down the middle of a blade. "I believe a leaf of grass is no less than the journey-work of the stars," said Walt Whitman. Look at the stirring of leaves, the corkscrew tendrils of a vine, touch the chipped bark of a stick. Notice how light changes the color of everything; I've seen pink telephone poles at dusk. Muse, watch, and compare what you see to something else. Play mind games with yourself. It will add to your stockpile of stories.

Go at it with what Charles Dickens called "the capacity to be pleased." This is a great phrase to tuck under your arm as you head out into the world to look around. You are going out to revive the powers of observation you had as a child, to retrieve an inheritance from your own childhood. What a wonderful thing to inherit from yourself. It will come back if you *want* it.

Watch for nature's exotica. Don't scrape in the kitchen when the dunes behind your house are flapping with migrating golden grosbeaks. Take the binoculars. Don't be consumed with taxes in March; fifteen minutes in the woods might turn up a trillium. When you get a cold snap, get out to see if green ice really exists. In the first nights of August, lie on your back and watch the falling stars. Appreciate, as the poet Richard Wilbur does, "the beautiful changes." You don't have to be on horseback in Montana or in scuba gear among the corals to find nature's marvels. Consider the hydraulics of a grasshopper, the spiraling line of a mosquito's flight, the sensuousness of moss. Go to the open window and turn your senses on a draft of air. Imagine that a molecule of Madame Curie's breath — or anyone's you admire — is mixed in with yours. Look for overlap, whimsical ideas, new edges to your thinking. This will develop your creativity.

Nature can be seen, no matter where you live. And it is not always pretty. It is a storm gathering blackly behind the trees or the skyscrapers; it is the sound of the wind moaning on your windows; it is the yellow, greasy sky of tornado weather.

I have a young friend in California named William who once showed me a wall crawling with snails. He told me his mother hated them. I could see why, they were shuddery things. He said he'd get a penny apiece if we picked them up, and he seemed to want to. So we carefully put about two hundred of them in a paper bag as we chatted, getting used to the slimy feel of them, tossed the bag into the full trash barrel, topped it, and forgot about them. In the morning, we found that the snails had lifted the lid somehow, a cooperative ooze, and had escaped onto the driveway, leaving little wet marks behind them, headed for the wall. There is story material in stuff like this. It doesn't have to be rosebuds to be inspiring.

Use the dark side of nature — "nature without its diadem," as Emily Dickinson called it — in your stories too. If you have experienced a natural disaster, seen lives disrupted, you can use it in a story. But remember to use it to search for meaning, as a way to feel alive. Life somehow goes on. Tell your child that the world has good and evil in it — through the metaphor of nature — but always look for the sprout of new life.

Observe People

Recently, I walked to the coffee store to buy some coffee beans, look around my neighborhood in the spirit of Dickens, and see what hit me. I followed my nose as I walked because this store has a roaster on the roof that fills the neighborhood with a dense trail of fragrance, more muscular than chocolate or bread. When I entered the store, there was a *fireman* in there, wearing a Darth Vader slicker with phosphorescent stripes on the sleeves and a huge, Napoleonic hat furled on his head. What a payoff for my small intention to look around; this would have snapped me out of any fog. The fireman was simply standing in line, no smoke, everyone was calm. His boots jingled as he walked out with some French Roast to the fire engine down the street.

I got my beans and started home, thinking about what I'd seen. I was charmed by the fireman's enormous hat, awed by his profession. I mused on "bravery," about how it must stand in line sometimes. I smelled the coffee in my arms, saw the wholesome blue sky overhead. Deciding to observe, I spotted a man in a station wagon taking a bite of an overflowing sandwich; a woman in black patent heels grabbing at the loose leash of her fluffy yellow dog; a man with a dirty towel hanging from his pocket walked by, reading *War Games Through the Ages*. After each one, I felt a zing of perception, the sense of an unexpected tidbit received, and fresh thoughts arose. I found myself imagining lives, holding up mental snapshots, inventing little films and flashbacks. I felt my throat catch with some of them, but I felt invigorated.

Perhaps it's the coffee or his training that gets the fireman going, but for me, in an inner way, it is the *seeing*. Seeing is not the kind of bravery it takes to save a child from a burning building, seeing is, rather, a kind of stand-in-line, mild form of bravery. When I keep my eyes open for glimpses of people and what they are doing, it feeds me with the energy, curiosity, and compassion I need for stories and just plain living.

Your stories will be more cruxed, more vivid, more shrewd if you take in people and human nature. Not much has changed since Micah envisioned beating our swords into plowshares; we're still animals. But we are also uniquely thinking and loving beings too, groping through the violence and brutishness with our minds aimed at transcendence, reaching for the higher ground. Watch for both aspects in the people around you.

To create living heroes, brave escapes, and sweet rewards, keep your eye on how faces and bodies express life. What you see will give you homemade storytelling power. Watch eyes, "the window to the soul." Notice the thrust jaw, the toothy breathing, the staccato voice of anger, the tearlessness of the worn-down will, the relaxed, steady mouth of a brave man or woman. Listen for sighs and what they signify. When happiness takes over, see the eyebrows perk, hear the high music of the voice. Try to see what motivates people to use their minds over their bodies: generosity, self-discipline, gratitude, thoughtfulness, to name some of my favorites. Of course there are other motivations too. Since I use fear, appetite, and curiosity as the motives that get my characters moving around, I try to watch people to see how they express these things. I try to watch with a capacity to be pleased, even if I notice something unpleasant. I figure it will make me wiser to see it, and if I am wiser I'll tell better stories. Fight bravely to keep your eyes open, and let your mind wander on what you see.

Because you have chosen to look for them, you will have at your narrative fingertips some closely observed details of human behavior to put into your stories. The giant scratches his nose when he tells a lie; the dragon passes gas to mark his territory; the birds toss maple whirligigs down on the cat to confuse her; the pioneer bathes in the river after crossing the mountains; the winner guzzles water straight from the faucet. Because you have observed people and nature, your imagination will hand some of it back to you in storytelling, delivering mysteriously just the right location for an adventure, just the right detail or gesture to enliven your hero and your tale.

Gathering In the Sparks

Just about the time I was to have a momentous birthday (five years later it doesn't seem so momentous, frankly), I heard the poet Robert Bly talking on the radio. He has a melodious voice, a nice timbre to it, pleasant to hear. He was talking about how when we are born, we have tremendous light within us. Babies come into the world full of a complete energy that is radiant and whole: 360 degrees of perfect light. He talked about the process of growing up and how, in order to do that, we have to shed some of this light. Abandon some sparks. We choose to do this, and society conspires, approves probably. When we are six or seven years old, Bly said, something happens in the species — we realize we have a certain gender, and certain kinds of choices become necessary. It becomes uncomfortable for boys among boys to play with dolls, difficult for girls to spend time building forts together in the backyard. Humanity divides. Around second grade it becomes difficult for boys and girls to be the playmates they used to be, preferring their own gender, shunning the other gender, declaring each other to be "nerds," "jerks," and so on.

As I listened to what Bly was saying about gender and time, I was reminded of the night before when my twins, aged six, a boy and a girl, were brushing their teeth together and squabbling about who was going to spit first. As the foam crept equally down their chins, they each had a reason why their gender had the privilege. My daughter bellowed, "Girls first!" And my son, shaking his toothbrush at her, said, "I was here before you. I'm bigger. If you spit first, I'll spit on you." What? Not my wonderful, distinct, affectionate twins. But yes, it *was* happening, even as their father did the dishes in the kitchen. My children were dropping remarks about the other gender as easily as they dropped their jackets on the kitchen floor after school. I could see Bly was right, and it made me shiver as a mother. I started having unsettling thoughts and was taken with a kind of sadness for it all, no matter what the cause, mine, theirs, society's. I had been feeling that my children's lives were getting away from me anyway; that I could no longer completely know them, as I had thought I had for the first few years. I was sorry for them, losing their wholeness. And, most of all, as my birthday loomed in those low February clouds, I was aggrieved for the light that I had spent, shed, thrown away, used up. I felt greedy about all these sparks that I had apparently let sputter out, go dead. I felt sorry for myself. Why does growing older always mean losing light? I didn't like it, even if it was true.

And then came Bly's wonderful comment. He said something like this. That as we end our twenties and thirties, with all that libidinous, gendered business of leaving home, falling in love, starting careers, after the heat and lust and joy of reproduction, as we sight the edges of our youth, we come to a turn, almost a U-turn, at plus or minus forty years of age. We go to an inward phase, begin to live inside more, become more androgynous — females more potent, males more nurturing; whatever it was of your natural-born "whole" self that you dropped by the wayside begins to come back. We start to retrieve some of the "other" we gave up over the years. He said, "We begin to gather in the sparks."

I have toyed with that phrase for years now, remembered literal lights of my childhood: the Big Dipper, candles, sparklers on the Fourth of July, moons shining on Lake Michigan, my father's cigarette embers on a cricketed summer night, fireflies in the long grass, my mother's pearl necklace when she would kiss me good night and go out, leaving a fragrance of fresh fingernail polish behind her. I've been retrieving these sparks and others — qualities in hibernation, unused searchlights — in order to be as whole as possible, to retrieve something of my original self.

Your imagination will come back and be strengthened as you pick up things you dropped along the path, as you go inward. You will be amazed that you really hadn't missed the insights, memories, images — of who you are and were — that are now coming back to you. You will wonder how you could have forgotten what you once knew, but you will treasure what comes and be grateful to have it home again.

Spirit, the Big Half of the Wishbone

As you keep your eyes open on nature, people, and yourself, with a capacity to be pleased, what will come flooding in will be booming, shining, imaginative material because you have opened the door to your spirit, the answer-finder, the part of you that seeks to *transcend* human nature, natural disaster, confusion, isolation, separation, and pain. The more this transcendent part of you is invigorated, the more meaning and appreciation you will find, and the more steam you will have to tell stories or do anything.

When I became a storyteller, I didn't really have any goals. I was playing with memory. I wanted to be like my father, who had created a charmer named Rainbow the Cat for me. I loved her spunk, her multicolored moods, her leaps and landings. I also wanted to be like my mother, who is anecdotal by nature, can make *any* description vivid, and had made my great-grand-parents' lives real to me: picnics beside the Pierce Arrow, the day Roosevelt closed her grandfather's bank, women in long dresses with strong opinions. But more than that, I wanted to go back to my children's world to share it with them, be there again, on the common ground of enchantment.

Thinking I was going back to my childhood during those first stories, I was in fact going farther. Over the years I have become aware that mysterious tidbits in ordinary bedtime stories often link me to a deeper humanity, larger than my own life span, wider than my family ties. I am linked to rich, red sagas, to the sweep and ping of nature, to ancient, universal wishes and themes, to a human family born in "oneness," the same stock, bone, and dreams. In the gentle air of the story, there is a species, a life form, a totality there in our little room — not just me and my children and our genes, but a miracle, an old, old story. This awareness is an intangible, exquisite sensation. Different from love or protectiveness, different from intellectual knowledge, it is a transcendent combination of the two — a feeling-awareness — a beautiful sense of kinship, continuance, and scope.

Like you, I have all the usual weights and tonnage

that the rest of the adult world experiences as a drag on the spirit, but when I tell a story, I rise, briefly, to beautiful heights. Like the breeze I can feel on my face without knowing where it comes from or where it goes, my spirit exists like the wind, invisibly filling the gaps in the story. As Annie Dillard says, "The gaps are the thing. The gaps are the spirit's one home." Your spirit has a very small voice, but it is stately and wise. I believe that as you tell stories, you will hear it.

When aimed at something you feel tenderly for, when summoned and focused by love, your imagination is your most eloquent spirit coming out of the blued or starry depths. It can deepen you with its energy, expand your respect and appreciation of life, and, at the very least, help you tell better tales to that little child of yours who already has so much to contend with.

Lullaby and Good Night

Storytelling captures and sets free again some of the meaning you have found in life, and often does it better than a lecture or a lesson or a speech permeated with abstract, slippery words. Children listen to stories; they understand the picture-language. After the tale is done, something lingers for your child to think about which affirms, encourages, and heartens. By hearing the emblematic tales that spring from your spirit and your love, your child will sense his or her own worthy being in your eyes, and perhaps sense a worthiness in the broader sweep of the human race. His or her tender longings, affections, wishes, curiosities, gripes, and sorrows — and your own — will be explored more richly in stories, night after night, because your child is not alone in his imagination, not alone in her spirit. You're there.

978-0-595-46298-8
0-595-46298-7

Made in the USA
Lexington, KY
26 March 2011